The Jonesport Raffle

Books by John Gould

The Jonesport Raffle

and numerous other
Maine veracities

researched and methodically arranged by
that pleasant humorist-philosopher with
a considerable local reputation, as well
as a profound sense of scholastic nicety,

JOHN GOULD

Illustrations by
EDWARD MALSBERG

Down East Books

Camden, Maine
Guilford, Connecticut

Down East Books

An imprint of Globe Pequot

Distributed by NATIONAL BOOK NETWORK

Copyright © 1969 John Gould
First Down East Books edition 2017

British Library Cataloguing in Publication Information available

Library of Congress Cataloging-in-Publication Data available

ISBN 978-1-60893-554-3 (paperback)
ISBN 978-1-60893-555-0 (e-book)

Printed in the United States of America

For THOMAS RUSSELL GOULD

. . . namesake of an illustrious folklorist, his great-great-grandfather. At the battlefield of Gettysburg, as the North and South were drawn up in array, General Joshua L. Chamberlain arrived on a horse and called out, "Is Tom Gould here?" "Right here, General!" he shouted, and raised an arm. "All right," said General Chamberlain, "then let the battle begin!" (Later that afternoon General Chamberlain came back, hunted Thomas up, and said, "All right, Tom, you've shot enough, you can have the rest of the day off.")

The Jonesport Raffle

The Jonesport Raffle

Truthfully, the existence and activities of the American Folklore Society, Inc., came only recently to my attention. I chanced upon a society publication and found in it the fine old down-east folklore story of the big raffle held at Jonesport. A professor had come to Maine through the generosity of a nice scholarship grant, and with excellent good sense had decided to do his research in Jonesport, which is an unspoiled fishing village where a pleasant vacation may be superimposed on scholasticism without attracting undue attention. This professor had located what he termed "a local humorist-philosopher with considerable reputation" and had persuaded him to talk onto a tape and thus record folklore.

Soon after I learned of this, a young fellow posing as a student came to call on me, and he said he was studying down-east speech and coastal folklore, and he wondered if I would recite a few ballads and *chansons de jest* to help him with his doctoral exegesis. It would help, he said, if I would do this in authentic Maine dialect. I started to tell him about the big raffle at Jonesport, but he stopped me and said *that* one was already recorded and in print — which I knew, anyway. As a local humorist-philosopher with considerable reputation, I thus had my eyes opened to new possibilities, and if professors and students may make grist of our ancient Maine doozies, I see no reason why the local humorist-philosophers shouldn't do as much.

Evidently, in the quest of down-east folklore, the tale of the Jonesport raffle ranks as a cultural achievement along with the Rosetta stone, the birth of Chaucer, and the invention of movable type — but we local humorist-philosophers never knew it. Had I known it a lifetime ago I could have set the thing down and become a wealthy Indiana professor, but my tendency was to hush the thing up. This professor, however, gave it new standing and new context, and received an academic ovation for his discovery. The story is about a man who sold tickets around town and raffled off his horse, and when the winner went with a halter to fetch his prize, he found the horse had been dead for a week.

To isolate this folklore in Jonesport is a high cultural achievement, because this horse has long been more ubiquitously deceased than even the charger of General Phil Sheridan. He has died and been raffled off in Freeport, Dexter, Berwick, Houlton, Waterford, Stratton, Machias, Perham, Edgecomb, Beddington, Cornish, Litchfield, Wilson's Mills, Freeman, and twice in Harmony. Jonesport, however, is about the best of all these places to spend the month of July.

A short time ago Dick Dyer said it had been a long, long time since he had heard anybody tell about the way to keep a horse from drooling. This is true. Maine people would as soon recite the Gettysburg Address to the Lincoln Society as new material. But the story is endemic and slumbering, and with a proper federal grant some persistent professor could easily dig it out and give it literary importance. It was, originally, an advertisement in *Home Comfort* magazine, and if you sent in fifty cents they would tell you how to stop your horse from drooling. All farm nags slobber some, so a lot of people sent in fifty cents. Back came the reply: teach him to spit.

Dick Dyer was answered by Red Cousins, who said, "Eyah, that's a good one, but I always liked the sure cure for potato bugs!" That, also, was an advertisement in *Home Comfort*, and if you sent in fifty cents they would tell you how to kill potato bugs. Back came two little wooden blocks marked A and B. The directions were to put the potato bug on block A and strike him with block B.

While we were on this tedious subject, not knowing at the time that we were innocently dabbling in the folklore profession, I had to come up with something, so I told about the skinny cat at the Scott Brook lumber camp. This cat was so skinny he came and went through a knothole in the cookshack wall. To keep the cat out, rather than climb up and plug the hole, the cook tied a knot in the cat's tail.

But now, you see, we find this is all folklore, nuggets from a rich vein — we didn't know that. Mrs. Hunter of South Hope, Mrs. Frazier of Cathance, Mrs. Randall of Phillips, Mrs. Gooding of Fairfield,

Mrs. Burnett of Lincoln, Mrs. Peabody of North
Yarmouth — these ladies didn't know it either. These
ladies were so fat that a fireman, bringing them down
a ladder, had to make two trips. Nor did Ed Grant,
who weaned his pet trout from water and then saw
the fish fall in the brook and drown. Or Charlie
Murch, who rode a dolphin up on shore from four
miles at sea and said it was kind of fun but he had
trouble keeping his hat on. Or Ken Lunt, who laid
stone wall all day and it took him three days to walk
back. He'd have laid more, but he had to fetch his
own rocks. Or Jim Bruce, who had an ungodly fight
with a she-bear and would pause in the tale to light
his pipe. The city sports would say, "Well, for gra-
cious-sake, Mr. Bruce — what happened?" Jim
would say, "She kilt me." Or Jim Hoar, who promised
his sports he would "call" a moose, and then with
ample theatrics shouted, "Here, Moosie, Moosie!"

And all this, and more, too, when it comes to research by out-of-state folklore talent, is subject to the
usual Maine discount. Well, who remembers Fred
Dunning, who kept store and had a sign out front,
"Waits Guessed"? Summer complaints, and probably some folklore students, figured Fred had mis-
spelled "weights," so they planned to have some fun
with him, and they'd lay a quarter on the counter
and ask him to guess their weights. Fred would put
the quarter in his pocket, look thoughtful, and say,
"Well, I guess you'll have to wait about eight minutes." Because the minute you insinuate an out-of-
stater, a summer complaint, a sport, a folklore student into the context, you have a new and artificial

situation. Charlie and Joe by themselves on a stone wall can talk to each other all day and create folklore by the mile. But the minute you stick a microphone to their faces, or ask them to talk dialect, they cease being folklorists and become actors. Then they tell you about the raffle of the dead horse. And that's the way it is with us salty down-east humorist-philosophers with considerable local reputation.

Did you hear the one about the horse with his head where his tail ought to be?

The Maine Schoolmarm

Lee Fields took his wife and fifteen children to Topsham Fair one time, and it cost ten cents to go in and look at the prize Holstein bull. Lee asked the man if they didn't have family rates, and the man says, "Are these fifteen children all yours?" "Yes, they are," says Lee. So the man says, "Well, you stand right where you are — I'm going to bring the bull out to see you!"

It is fairly easy to trace down folklore of this kind. Somebody is always saying, "You ought to go over and talk to so-and-so — he'll tell you more stories in one afternoon than you can write up in a year!" This sounds good.

"Get him to tell you about the time his wife fed the dead pig!"

I suppose a folklore student would trot right over, but I've always avoided such visits. Occasionally, in sour-pickle time, I've hunted up one of these sawmill philosophers, and he's always turned out to be a sane, intelligent, cultured, kindly man with no desire to foist prize bulls and dead hogs on me. I remember Jimmie Hunt, who was recommended as a fine source by a dozen well-intentioned friends. I called on him and saw his college diploma on the kitchen wall, and we spent the afternoon discussing the origins of Roosevelt's political philosophy. Then there was Roger Maxwell, who fished fifty lobster traps with a dory and could say the wittiest things to summer folks who thought he wasn't quite bright. Well, Roger had studied law, and one of his classmates finally got on the Supreme Court. Roger used to take his notes, look up citations, and write his opinions for him. Roger had about as much folklore as a moon rocket.

There is a wealth of lore in the Maine word "schoolmarm." It doesn't mean what you think. A fellow could come along with more degrees than a Masonic thermometer, and he could research "schoolmarm" until his grant ran out, and he wouldn't have it in its rich, total beauty. You have to go back to the days of sail, when half of Maine was at sea. Children were born in mid-ocean and grew up afloat. The state provided free education, but how did a boy on a three-year voyage to the Chiny Seas get to school on time? Very simple; the maritime interests effected a law that if children were unable to attend school, the state should send teachers to them. Thus every wife and mother who took her brood to sea became a public-school teacher. Every day she taught her children from books sup-

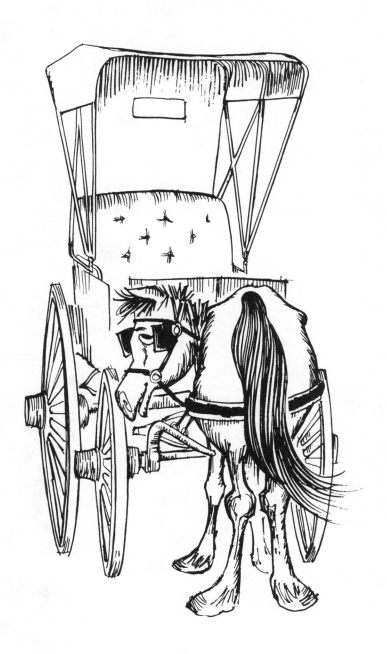

plied by the town, and according to a work schedule that kept up with the real teachers back home. When the ship arrived back in Maine the mother put in her bill for her time, and the town paid her for teaching her own children. The children, of course, could pass the little tests given for graduation, but they had also picked up pidgin English and ten other languages, could keep a manifest, and do celestial navigation, and a great many other topics which the landlubbers hadn't mastered had crossed their paths.

Originally, this provision for "sending a teacher" was meant solely for the seagoing communities, but the law was worded broadly, and in the next generation the state began letting light into the swamps, and the great Paul Bunyan era began. Paul, you know, was born in Maine. All at once Maine was loaded with remote lumber camps, and conversations about Timbuctoo, Valparaiso, Bombay, and Marseilles were shifted to conversations about equally romantic places named Letter M, and Location Four, and Gatchell's Grant, and Ten Mile Place. There were women and children in the vast north woods, and the old Maine law was still on the books, so somebody said, "Send us a teacher!" In some lumber camps mothers did teach their own and others' youngsters, but mostly there came up the professional schoolmistress, schoolmadam, schoolmarm.

You can't, today, get anything of the situation on tape. Lumber was cut and moved on snow, and winter was snow time. What kind of woman would sign up to buckboard and canoe far into the wilderness to earn a pittance thumping spelling into the heads of timberjack children, in a log schoolroom buried in drifts? Even the Peace Corps, which makes agony sound attractive, couldn't glamorize this. But women came to do it, and they went to pole backhouses at forty-five degrees below zero, and they ate pork and beans with indubitable interruptions of geography recitations, and they earned all they got. Even a folklorist would think on these people and then weep bitter tears for modern city teachers who have ten degrees in social reform and want twenty thousand dollars a year with fringes. The only benefit a Maine lumber-camp schoolmarm got was to wait for June and go home in a canoe to have a hot bath in a tub.

Now, every so often an old pine tree will survive an early injury and grow into two tops. The trunk will run up maybe twenty feet, and then there is a crotch, above which two trunks continue. Such a pine is useful for lumbering, usually, only up to the crotch, and the tops go to waste. And to some original lumberjack with a reputation for humor, unquestionably, the sight of a pine tree that seemed to wave two legs in the air suggested a schoolmarm. A schoolmarm, in Maine timber lingo, is not a schoolmistress, but a tree that has a crotch. One lumber company, listing what shall be harvested, has posters that say, ". . . and all schoolmarms regardless of size." There isn't a chopper in the Maine woods doesn't know what that means.

So you have a single word derived from two centuries of seafaring and logging — a single word packed with a whole saga of lore. From the mother sitting by a taffrail in the Indian Ocean asking her child to spell "phthisic," to the girl in the lumber camp making the youngsters name the continents. Even to the short-legged Canuck who leaned on his peavey, looked up at the pine, and with hearty woods humor said, "Moncree! A schoolmarm!"

So you don't always get the folklore from the people who can tell more stories in an afternoon than you can write up in a year. The dead pig? Oh . . .

This fellow was going into the woods to work for the winter, and he rigged a chute from the kitchen sink shelf so his wife could slosh down slops and wouldn't have to go outside to feed the pig. He came home in March and found the pig had died months ago and was buried in swill.

I trust you see what I mean.

Prairie Post Holes

A folklore student from the Middle West was perplexed by a story he researched in Maine, and it took me a little time to figure out why he failed to include it in his report. Well, a sailor was sitting in a barroom in Bangor telling a story, and just then a man stuck his head in the door and called, "Tide serves — *Elizabeth Farwell* about to sail!" At this the sailor jumped up, boarded the *Elizabeth Farwell,* and when he came back to the barroom in Bangor he went to the same table, took the same chair, and said, "Now, as I was saying . . ."

The problem of the folklore student, of course, is lack of knowledge of the old sailing days, when ships like the *Elizabeth Farwell* went down the Penobscot River on voyages that lasted from two to three years. Swift narration, a desideratum of all primitive literature, thus must not be too swift for the student. Another story that has had difficulties with the modern practitioner is about buying the wind. This, like the dead horse, is found almost everywhere. Cap'n Esau Bibber sat in the same spot in the Indian Ocean for three weeks without a breath of wind, in what Mainers call a "flat-arse calm," and he got tired of it. So he flipped a coin in the ocean and yelled, "Sell me a quarter's worth o' wind, goddam ye!"

Immediately the sky lowered and a typhoon struck him. With his masts overside and his decks littered with scraps of canvas and twisted lines, Cap'n Esau said, "If I'd-a knowed wind was so cheap, I'd not-a bought so much!"

I can report to you that this story has been cleaned up. A generation ago Cap'n Esau bought a shilling's worth of wind, not a quarter's worth. Even as recently as a generation ago some British coin words were used in Maine for United States money, and the shilling lasted longest. As late as the 1920's my grandfather would give me twenty-five cents, a quarter, and he would say, "Stop in at Bailey's and get me a harness buckle with this shilling." He knew it was a quarter and he knew it wasn't a shilling — but the word had come down from his boyhood and his father's boyhood. The reason the folklorists have changed from shilling to quarter is pure academic fallacy — they thought shilling didn't sound right. What they don't know is that it wasn't shilling in the first place, and that shilling was substituted long ago for another word that sounded even worse — farthing.

Early Mainers pronounced it "fart'in'." And a farthing was merely the smallest negotiable coin — the least amount. Fart'in' became shilling for reasons of nicety, and shilling became quarter because it sounded more Maine-ish. Both changes are an academic absurdity. The whole point of the story depends on the smallness of the coin, the cheapness of the wind. If you toss a quarter when there are dimes, nickels, and cents available, you are spoiling the point. Let us sincerely hope scholarship doesn't keep pace with inflation until some ancient mariner heaves over a five-dollar bill.

All Maine coastal folklore requires some special knowledge to "piecen out" the point. You need to realize, for instance, that a Monhegan Island story doesn't originate on the island, but is usually thought up by somebody on the mainland to poke fun at the place. All Monhegan Island stories are told, as well, about Loud's Island, Matinicus, and so on. There are a great many stories about postponing funerals because of rough seas and they couldn't bring the body to the main. The point being that you can't dig much of a grave on those rocky islands. Or, about sending in for lumber to make a casket. One yarn is about the sad grandchild, eyes swollen from weeping, who was sitting on the floor right beside Grammie — at last silent in death. Having no trees at hand, they wrapped the old girl in sailcloth and tied her around with pot warp. Right at the saddest part of the funeral services this granddaughter burst out into riotous laughter, uncontrolled hysterics.

"What in the world ever made you do such an awful thing?" they asked the child afterwards, and she answered, "I couldn't help it — all at once I got a picture of Grammie scuddin' into hell in a reefed mains'l."

A folklorist, and a very fine one, somehow translated this into a "close-hauled mainsheet," possibly fancying that a sheet and a winding-sheet have about the same sound, but scarcely anybody on Monhegan Island has made this error up to a late hour. I get the impression pedagogues west of Pittsburgh sometimes get the rudder mixed with the bowsprit. Henry Beston said one time, "There is no culture west of Framingham!"

There is one Monhegan Island story that has contributed generously to folklore, being a jump-off. It has to do with Sim Simmons's well. Sim, after a long career as a Monhegan lobsterman, decided to sell out and move to the mainland, where his old age would be more comfortable and he could have plumbing. He had no trouble selling his place, but he reserved his well. He found a pleasant house on the main, and moved his effects across in his lobster boat. Now, the special knowledge needed to appreciate all this is the great scarcity of good drinking water on these outermost islands. Sim was lucky to have an excellent well on the island, and he didn't want to give it up. So after he got everything else moved, he went back and took up his well. He got it on his boat and lashed it firmly, and struck out. About halfway across he struck a tide churn, and the boat pitched so that a line parted and his well rolled overboard.

He got a line on it, luckily, and in spite of heavy swells he towed it into Port Clyde and beached it out. He got it to his new house all right, and set it up — but always after that the water was salty.

This story may be considered the foundation for the whole galaxy of well and hole stories which sprang up almost at once. The peak of the industry was reached when the Newton Newkirk Enterprises took over the Consolidated Post Hole Corporation of America, and practically every old well in Maine was uprooted to keep the machinery going. This company made holes for any purpose — from tunnels in the Alps to a neat package of holes for a cribbage board. Every hole was guaranteed unconditionally not to bend, buckle, or break, with a complete money-back offer. All manner of raw materials were tried, but best of all was a Maine well, kiln-dried and treated. Over thirty-eight thousand abandoned wells were recut in the one turning mill alone at Jackman, Bingham, Abbott Village, Shirley Mills, Guilford, and so on. Availability of high-quality holes at honest prices inaugurated the entire Swiss cheese industry. St. Andrews Golf Club sent for eighteen custom-built holes, and these were double-lined and are still in use. And Maine post holes fenced the nation. At one time an abandoned quarry on Vinalhaven Island was being made into macaroni holes at the rate of over three hundred thousand miles a day.

All, of course, stemming from the original story of Sim Simmons's Monhegan Island well. Harold Spinney of the town of Industry used to tell of the time he went to Nebraska to the wheat harvest and tied bags on a huge combine that was drawn by twelve mules. One day the mules took a fright and ran away, and they went three and a half miles along a barbed-wire fence before they could be stopped.

Harold tied the bags, and he ought to know — he said that in that time they mowed, threshed, winnowed, and bagged thirty-eight bags of barbed-wire fence staples, but that not a single Maine-made post hole was dislodged or damaged in any way. Harold brought one home with him to prove it, and he had it in his living room. Fifty years later it was just as straight and sound as the day it was made.

How Peabody Perished

The authentic story of the man who froze to death in the snowbank is found in all sixteen counties of Maine, and may be regarded as the typical way of treating death and burial in ballads and folklore. There is usually some reluctance to give all details, because some of the family may still be living or there are innocent people to protect, but this may be only because nobody was exactly sure of what happened anyway. But there is little of the Barbary Allen hey-nonny-nonny touch throughout Maine, and the general attitude may be shown by the sign on the entrance of the cemetery at Randolph, which says, "One Way Street."

The Franklin County version is a good one. The Pulsifers had settled in for a pleasant Saturday evening, it being February and the barrel of new cider having accomplished its days. There were three Pulsifers — Nat, Thomas, and Peabody. They lived bachelor fashion in a large frame house just outside town, and they had many friends because of their cider. On this Saturday evening a number dropped in, and during the early hours it came off to snow hard. The party and the snow continued for some time — in fact, until about Tuesday. At some time, nobody could recall just when, Peabody Pulsifer got up and went outdoors, although he did not happen to state any reason. Several remembered definitely that he went out. When he did not return in a day or so, somebody stepped out to see if he was all right, and he could not be found. They called to him from the porch, but he did not answer.

But when the party broke up and the guests reluctantly insisted that they must go, lingering on the doorsteps to say farewell, a leg was noticed sticking out of the snowdrift, and investigation revealed it belonged to Peabody. With great sadness they withdrew him, and they found he had frozen to death in a great curved-up position, like a crescent moon. There was some discussion as to what might have brought on this dismal end, but nobody could think of any specific reason, and they fell to discussing what they could do now for poor Peabody. It occurred to them that persons who had not been at the party, such as a deputy sheriff, might not understand readily, so they decided to bring Peabody into the house, put him in bed, and hope the affair would pass as natural causes. This they did, and then somebody went and told the sheriff.

The sheriff came with the medical examiner, and they were both amazed to see Peabody resting comfortably, although extinct, under a carefully smoothed quilt, with his head up eighteen inches off the pillow. At this point the story takes off in any number of directions and may be embellished at will. In some versions a murder trial develops into a considerable comedy of errors, but the more artful folklorists usually leave it right by the bedside — the thoughts of Peabody in midair being sufficient.

Anguish and despair are not common in Maine laments. A man is said to be so crooked that when he dies they'll just screw him in the ground. And there's the critique of the poor soil in the town of Bowdoin — a load of manure always precedes the hearse into the cemetery to enrich the soil and assist the soul in rising. Epitaphs worth study abound, perhaps the best one being "I told you I was sick." Along the coast a favorite graveyard story has to do with the sea captain embalmed in rum — as was Captain John Paul Jones, if memory serves.

This sea captain took sick in a far port of call, and realizing that his end was nigh, he made the sailors promise to carry his body home to Maine, where he might be laid to rest in the family lot. They did so, and forthwith coopered his remains into a hogshead of rum, after which they completed the voyage and finally got back to Maine. The obsequies were held, and they lowered the hogshead of rum, captain and all, into the grave. And they have always said that on a warm June evening you can still smell the rum.

Sometimes, but not always, you get an expanded version of this story, in which it develops that the old sea captain was really a smuggler, and that his vessel had nothing aboard whatever except hogsheads of rum. The sailors, naturally, got the hogsheads mixed up, and they never did bury the captain in his family lot. They just buried a hogshead of rum. What became of the hogshead in which the captain was coopered is not stated, but it makes something to think about.

Murder and suicide, often the same thing in Maine, must not be neglected. Sometimes it's complicated, such as the simple murder on the Isles of Shoals, which degenerated into a major dispute between Maine and New Hampshire as to which state had jurisdiction — neither wanted the murder, but each wanted the Isles of Shoals. Or cases are quickly settled, such as the man who was hit on the back of the head with an ax, dismembered, and thrust into a barrel of hog victuals. Clearly, he had taken his own life in a fit of despondency. In another instance of involuntary suicide, two young men from out of state were arrested for murder by an absurd police officer who wanted to get his name in the papers, and for a short time it looked as if Maine's

long record of clean homicidal folklore was to be upset. But the court ruled that these people were tour-
ists, and if Maine held them for murder or man-
slaughter it might make people skittish about coming
into the state, and hurt the summer business. The
men were discharged, with apologies. Generally
speaking, in Maine, it's murder whenever the Boston newspapers want photographs, and otherwise it's
suicide.

Many years ago a gentleman from Boston who
owned a rubber factory came up to Maine on a
hunting trip, and he got lost in the woods. It was
coming on winter, and things froze up, and everybody who knew about this remarked that it was a
tarnation shame, etc., and they felt sorry for the wife.
Well, with customary tact the Maine police and
judiciary dismissed the whole matter. But one of the
Boston papers decided the social season was otherwise dull and a little spice and pepper would help,
so they sent a man up to Jackman to "investigate"
the murder of this unfortunate hunter, who was now
described as a tycoon. The reporter successfully
sowed and then reaped, and in a few days had
erected the whole thing into a monumental murder
mystery which went on and on.

For instance, the reporter would say to the sheriff,
"I say, don't you think it would be a good idea to
use bloodhounds?"

"Oh, I don't know," the sheriff would reply. "Been
a lot of snow, and we don't know which way the
fellow went, and I wouldn't know where to get any
bloodhounds."

The reporter would say, "Well, if you had some bloodhounds you'd use them, wouldn't you?"

"Oh, I suppose so — maybe."

The next morning the Boston newspaper had a big headline, "Sheriff To Use Bloodhounds." And, of course, the editor of the paper had arranged for a crate of bloodhounds to arrive by express that same day. The next day the Boston paper had a headline, "Bloodhounds Used In Tycoon Murder Search."

This went on all winter, and along in the spring they found the fellow's body where he'd got lost and frozen to death. It was a valiant try, but it's pretty hard to make murder stick. Maine has its own way. After all, you must bear in mind that we had a rip-tearing war on our hands up here years ago, back when we were fighting over the Aroostook frontier, and we hardly programmed the conflict according to the established rules. The only casualty after all the hullabaloo was a poor unheroic devil who gave his life to his country by getting run over by a wagon.

A Few Appropriate Words

Nothing like the Loch Ness monster has ever been reported in Maine, although Barnabas Griffin once hooked a cusk in Moosehead Lake which ran to considerable size. Barney hauled in eight feet of the fish before he came to the eye, and he got frightened and cut the line. Speaking of Moosehead Lake, Earle Doucette told some

golfers one time that he could drive a golf ball fourteen miles, and they indicated disbelief. Earle picked
a day when Moosehead Lake was frozen and
the wind was brisk out of the northwest, and had
no trouble at all. Putts up to thirty-five miles have
been made.

Years ago there was a fish-story contest in Mon-
tana, and a Maine man sent an entry. The prize was
to be a flyrod, but he said he never used a rod — he
hid on the bank and clubbed the trout with a
ball bat when they came up to pick blueberries. He
won the prize, and the Associated Press was
careful to assure readers that this was a "tall story."
But truthfully, it is nothing to see men with ball
bats lined up along a brook in Maine — not
for taking trout, but for self-defense. The vicious
man-eating trout of Franklin County have been
known to drive a man up a tree, and then jump at
his feet. This is what happened to Reinhard Bolster.
He was from Connecticut. He was alone, but another party down the stream heard his frantic cries
and rushed to his assistance, too late. He was fishing
Cue-Ball Pool, a fairly deep hole in the North Branch
just above Eustis, which is notorious for its man-
eating trout and is consequently avoided by the na-
tives. This is the pool where Benedict Arnold lost so
many men on his expedition of 1775, but the
military historians have erroneously ascribed the
tragedy to the weather. Mr. Bolster, being innocent
of the danger, was unarmed and carried only his
bottle of lunch and a three-piece rod. He must have
shouted as soon as he saw the trout coming for him,

and he turned and climbed the nearest tree, which was a small poplar. When help arrived, the savage claw marks of the ravenous fish were found a good eight feet up the tree, but Mr. Bolster was gone. Those who had heard him cry and came a-running were so awed by the gruesome fate of the man that they kneeled a moment in prayer, and then erected a rude cross.

Three seasons later, in the fall spawning time, one of the trout in this same pool charged ashore and made a savage lunge at Joseph Arsenault, a registered Maine guide from Stratton, who was hunting deer. Joseph felled him with a single shot, and was astonished to find the trout wearing a necktie which was afterwards positively identified as Mr. Bolster's.

It was Joseph Arsenault, incidentally, who was guiding the two priests on that same stream one time, and related the incident of the whiskey. One of the priests tied into a small trout at Sherampus Falls and greatly enjoyed the thrill of landing him. When he got him off the hook and into his creel, the other priest reached in his hip pocket and drew forth a pint of whiskey, saying, "I think this calls for a little celebration!" He removed the cap and passed the bottle to the priest who had just landed the trout, and because his hand was wet the bottle slipped and fell in the stream, and broke on a rock.

At this, he turned to Joe and said, "I wonder, Joseph, if you would say a few words appropriate to the occasion?"

This same Joseph was sitting in a rocking chair

on the porch of the Mégantic Club at Chain of Ponds one afternoon, and he noticed a deer moving on the sheer ledges of the Height of Land across the lake. He pointed out the deer to some of the members, and one of them said he would sure like to be near enough for a clean shot at a rauncher like that. Joe said he could hit him from here. Well, the upshot was that they brought a rifle and told Joe to prove it. Joe rested the barrel on the porch railing, and when he got a line he raised the muzzle about a foot and touched her off. It was a long shot, so Joe had the gun all cleaned and stood in the corner before the deer gave a jump and fell dead. The members were amazed, and never failed to tell of Joe's marksmanship.

Joe, of course, had to go down and put a boat in, and row across the lake and climb up on the mountain to get the deer. He found the deer had been hit right between the eyes. But it was such a far distance and it took him so long to get there, that the meat had spoiled.

Little has been heard in recent years about the musical fish of Spear Pond, partly because oceanography has discovered so many similar things, and what was once regarded as folklore is now scientific fact. It was in 1888 that Prof. Bradley Wheelock of Harvard College discovered the bass orchestra in Spear Pond, and while his first reports were not fully credited at once, the man's scholastic standing was so above reproach that his findings could not be ignored. He was not, actually, an icthyologist; his field was Greek and Latin, and he

used to come to Spear Pond, with his wife and daughter, for a July vacation. Mrs. Wheelock and her daughter did not relish this rural retreat, preferring the gay life of Cambridge, but they indulged the professor and amused themselves as best they could. It was his custom to row a boat out on the pond and then drift aimlessly as he read Horace and Livy, etc.

On this particular evening he had drifted into the cove on the south shore, farthest from the cottage, and had come to rest in some reeds where the sandy bottom was visible in about four feet of water. He chanced to look overside, and saw a black bass swim by with a mandolin around his neck on a strap. At the time he thought nothing of it and returned to his book. But soon he was astonished, in that place, to hear a clear voice which said (in French), "S'il vous plaît, messieurs, commencez par le deuxième double-eff!" Immediately the entire cove was bathed in the sweet concord of lovely music, and the professor recognized it as Mendelssohn's "Spring Song." Dumbfounded, Prof. Wheelock saw that he was surrounded by a complete orchestra of fish. Afterwards was rendered Rubenstein's Melody in F and then the overture to *William Tell,* and the concert was finished by Beethoven's Unfinished.

(There was an exciting quartet rendition, also, which was composed of a first tuna, second tuna, barracuda, and bass.)

The next evening Prof. Wheelock brought his wife and daughter, and they were entranced. Particularly Mrs. Wheelock, who was a patroness of the Boston Symphony and something of a student of music. When Prof. Wheelock later transcribed his notes and published his monograph, it made something of a stir. He was relieved of his classical teaching soon after to devote his full time to the Spear Pond Symphony, and for a number of years he was a familiar figure in that vicinity. But he long ago ceased to come, and in the meantime his early observations have been superseded by the more methodical methods of the oceanographers.

Perley the Poacher

"I'll tell you the saddest man I ever knew — it was Perley Goodwin over to Parkman. He was the biggest poacher in Maine, but he never got arrested for anything he did. He got arrested for everything else, but it was always a plant or a mistake. They was always after him, and they never got him. I say 'sad,' because the poor devil spent a good part of his time being accused of things he never did, but he'd done so many things that was worse, he had no right to complain. Like the time he was sitting in his front room reading a magazine, and he heard a gun go off out in the road. He runs out, and here in the dark somebody he never saw before sticks a gun in his hand and runs like hell. There was a deer dead right on the highway, and just then the warden steps up. Perley paid two hundred dollars for night hunting and hunting out of season, and he couldn't keep the deer and they took the man's gun away from him. It was sad.

"Best story about Perley is the time his wife poached a deer. He used to have a camp up on Mayfield Hill, and every fall he'd take two-three sports in at a time and get them a deer. Along the last of August, Perley went up to his camp to check it and see that everything was ready for fall, and he took a pail to pick some raspberries. He put a new seat on the outhouse where the porkies had chawn it, and steadied up the flue-pipe, and he picked his pail of raspberries, and by the time he got home back in Parkman he was completely bushed out and ready for bed. Couldn't hardly keep his eyes open to eat supper, and as soon as he could he ups to bed.

"Well, his wife — Clarice was her name, she was about as pretty as anybody you'll ever clap an eye on, and red-headed — his wife puts things away and washes the dishes, and she mends a few socks or something, and finally she starts for bed, too. Oh, I forgot to mention — Perley is one of these red-blooded jokers who sleeps in the raw. Never wears anything to bed. So he's pounding them off and is away over the hill in sweet dreams, and Clarice tippy-toes into the bedroom as quiet as fog coming off a millpond, and she takes off her clothes and stands there bare-arse looking out the window in the moonlight. It is a beautiful evening, and she sees a deer standing in the garden eating at a row of carrots. So all quiet, she reaches in the corner and she picks up Perley's Winchester .45–70, and she draws a bead on the deer through the window, and she touches her off. Wham!

"Well — you can surmise what this sounds like to Perley. He bounds out of bed and trots all around the bedroom, still mostly asleep, and in his groggy condition he catches sight of his beautiful wife standing there with a rifle, and he assumes she is trying to murder him in his bed. In that flicker of time betwixt sleep and wake the poor slob gets quite a scare. But Clarice realizes immediately what's going on in his befuddled mind, and she shouts, 'I shot a deer!' This clears everything up, and by now Perley is awake, so he goes down the front stairs and out onto the front porch with the idea of proceeding around back to look at the deer. Now you got to visualize all this, taking into account that Perley is stark naked, that there is a moon, that his wife is also stark naked, and she has a gun in her hands. Because it was Perley's usual bad luck that just as he came larruping out the front door a truck went by out on the road, and it was Tyler Bradshaw, the warden supervisor over to Hartland. Tyle was just out cruising around, but you've always got to allow for coincidence. Well, sir — you can imagine what this must have looked like to Tyler Bradshaw! He sees Perley come out like a whippet, and right behind him his wife with a gun. Tyle is out of his truck in a second, and sizing things up he yells, 'Don't shoot, Clarice! Don't shoot!'

"Perley is no fool, so he also sizes things up, and he begins to cry out, and he shouts, 'Don't shoot, Clarice — I didn't mean nothing! Spare me, spare me! Forgive me!' and so on. Well, by this time

Clarice has also sized things up, and she's no fool either, and she cocks the gun and she yells, 'I've had enough of you, you low-down so-and-so!' and she lays it right on, using a few words that caused Tyler Bradshaw to blush, and when Perley turned the corner of the house, she took right behind him. And Tyle, he took behind them both.

"Well, the upshot was that Tyle ran Clarice down, and he knocked the rifle out of her hands and he threw his arms around her and pinned her to the house, and then Perley came back and pleaded for mercy and whimpered a good bit, and they put on such a good act that Tyler never suspected a thing. He hung around until they'd kissed and made up, previous to which they'd been invested with what they'd been divested of, and Clarice made some coffee and Tyle had a piece of pie. He made them both promise to love, honor, and obey, and he left. After he was gone Perley dressed the deer, and he told me afterwards it went to one hundred and eighty pounds and Clarice had slugged him right in the heart.

"But the sad part is to picture Perley, standing there in the moonlight looking at the game warden fondling his naked wife, and Perley was in no position to object. He couldn't say one word. Just had to stand there and whimper. Another time I know about, Perley stepped out to the hovel just before he went to bed, to check the horse, and he got the horse a drink. He picked up a pail and went down to the brook behind the hovel, and he was just about to dip a pail of water when somebody

stepped out of the bushes and dumped a whole sag-
net of smelts right into his pail. Perley told me it
was too dark to see who the fellow was, but he remembers how those smelts shined in the night.
Well, this fellow had seen the game warden
coming, and all at once he had to get rid of his
smelts, and there was Perley with a pail. Perley had
probably poached more smelts out of that brook in
his time than any other living man, without getting
caught, and now when he wasn't smelting at all he's
ordered into court. He paid. Perley always bellied
up and paid. But it was sad, all the same, to get
caught doing something you always did, when you
weren't doing it. Perley says he's the only man with a
fish-and-game crime record for watering a horse.

"They were always after him. There'd be wardens
behind every bush, and Perley didn't dare throw
a matchstick down or they'd have yanked him
in for littering. He knew it, and he never tripped up.
Although one time he overlooked a small item. He
was in the woods and he heard somebody yell, and
he found this man with a heart attack. He was sitting
by a stump and his friend was fanning him with his
hat, and Perley comes out of the puckerbrush and
sees that his man needs a doctor. So Perley picks
him up, lugs him down to the road, and off
they go in the friend's automobile for help. The
story has a happy ending, in a way, because they
got the man to a doctor and he came out of it all
right. But it also has a sad ending, because when
Perley picks up the fellow he still has his gun in his
hand; he clutched it all the way and groaned and

carried on, and this is where Perley made a mistake. When they got to the doctor's office the game wardens arrested Perley for having a loaded gun in the car. It's the truth. Perley was always philosophical about these things — he'd mention all the times he drove all over the country road, hunting with a gun loaded and sticking out the window, and no game warden was ever smart enough or quick enough to catch him, so he didn't get fussed up just because an errand of mercy backfired. But it was sad to see Perley paying a fine because he drove an ailing cardiac to the doctor's. Eyah — Perley would say, 'They didn't catch me fair; they didn't catch me fair!' And that's about the size of it."

Dr. Willoughby's Daughter

[*This story has been isolated at Sebago, Rangeley, Moosehead, Grand, Chamberlain, Mattagammon, and Eagle.*]

"Well, I had the summer complaint that season — bad enough to doctor for it — so I took things easy and I didn't get in on much of the fishing. But there is a silver lining to every dark cloud and every misfortune has its own reward, and this protracted illness gave me time to become an inventor, and I gave the world one of its greatest boons.

"You recall Dr. Willoughby from Philadelphia. A fine old gentleman he was. He was a kidney specialist, and he tied all his own flies. He and his wife came every July for the whole month, and they always insisted on having me. I guided them year after year. He was the best hand with a dry fly I ever see, and I never knew him to kill a fish. He'd hook one and play it, and then let it go. 'There!' he'd say. 'Now let's get another one!' His wife loved to fish just as much as he did, and I've seen it so cold and blowing you couldn't keep a line on the water, and she'd come down a good deal more ready to go than I was. Wonderful woman. Well, this summer I was having my troubles, so I wrote and told them I wouldn't be available. They wrote right back, telling me how sorry they was, and would I find them somebody. Said they relied on my judgment. I got Charley Coombs, he was a good man, so they were all set and they came on the Fourth of July. I stirred around and went down to the lodge to shake hands with them, and I met their daughter.

"I never knew they had a daughter. She was the prettiest young lady you can imagine, about twenty-two—twenty-three, black hair and black eyes, and a personality you wouldn't find one in a million. She hung onto my hand and said Daddy and Mummie had spoken of me so much she felt she had always known me, and they told of such wonderful times in Maine that she just had to come up finally and see for herself. Well, it turned out she didn't care for fishing. Charley Coombs must have been glad when he found that out, because he had to use a big boat for four, and with three lines out he was in a snag a good part of the time. So the girl stayed ashore and

Charley took the doctor and his wife out fishing, and that made it some better for Charley. Then it turned out that the girl was an artist. She'd take her paints and set up a frame thing, and she could turn out real good pictures. Trees, best of all. She could make a pass with a brush, and there would be a spruce tree you'd swear you could walk right up to and pick off a chew of gum. One day I found her by the icehouse, and I sat on a stump and watched, and it was just unbelievable. Anyway, I said, 'You ought to go down the lake, or maybe up the river, and you'd find some pretty spots to paint.' The upshot being that I said I'd take her in a canoe if I chanced to feel up to it, and so on, and that's just what I did. Tell you the truth — being around that lovely young lady kind of perked me up, and besides that it was educational. And I paddled her around, and every night we'd exhibit the new picture we'd done, and Dr. and Mrs. Willoughby were pleased. Well, it bothered them a mite that their only daughter didn't take to fishing, but they could see she was having a fine vacation all the same. Dr. Willoughby told me, 'I'm going to pay you guide's wages for being so kind to her,' but I said no, I was having a good time and he didn't owe me a thing. He did give me a tip, though. Anyway, one day I says to her, 'I'm going to set you in by the big rock at Teakittle Brook, and I want you to paint me a picture that I can have for myself. That'll be my guide's pay.' She says fair enough, and that's where we went, and that's where it all happened.

"You know the spot — the brook comes out all white water and swirls into the lake right around the big rock. One of my favorite places. You can look at that swirl different times of day and see different colors that you don't get anyplace else, and the minute this girl set eyes on it she could see it was a challenge. She made me move in and out, putting the canoe in every possible position, and finally she says, 'I want to do it from right here!' So I held the canoe right where she says, and she gets out her paints and goes to work. I couldn't see what she was doing because of the way she faced, but she got absorbed in it and she stuck right with it until I got some tired of holding that canoe steady. Maybe two hours, and then she says, 'Mr. Knight — I'm afraid I'll have to trouble you to put me ashore.'

"I had to go myself, so I pulled in on the beach and she went up in the bushes one way and I walked down the other, and all at once I heard the most ungodly wail out of her, and it froze my marrow, it was so full of agony and pain. I bounded back and headed up through the bushes, and she kept screaming so I had no trouble finding her, and I'm telling you — it was one terrible thing!

(At this point in the narration a pipe is always filled and lit, a cat is let in or out, a stick needs to be added to the fire.)

"Well — to resume: That girl had stepped into the puckerbrush and had selected a retiring situation suitable for what she was about, and she had lifted her skirt and hunkered down for the business

at hand, and by the saddest misfortune ever to de-
scend on mortal female, she had scooched right over
a bull porcupine sleeping in the weeds! Words can-
not describe the horror. That porcupine had slapped
his tail right on her punky-poo with all the vigor at
his command, and had thus caused her to wail as I
have related. When I came charging up she was
holding her skirts high around her middle in a
manner that filled me with wonder, because at that
instant I didn't know why she was doing it, but then I
see this pork-pick lumbering away and figured
things out. All maidenly modesty was forgot, and I
looked the girl over after I got her quieted down, and
I can honestly say that I never see nothing like it
before nor since. Never. I assured her the discomfort
would prove temporary, and as if I was a doctor I
bowed and said, 'if you will permit me, I'll operate!'

"So I did. I got her down on the beach, and I
tipped the canoe up to give her something to lay
on, and I picked up a couple of fresh-water clamshells and made me some tweezers. She laid herself
belly-down on the canoe, her butt up so the sun was
giving me a good light to work by. I would put the
clamshells to a quill, tweeze it out, and she would
whimper. Poor thing. Then I'd get another. She had
seventy-nine needles all told, and I laid them out one
by one on the canoe and kept count. And about the
time I was getting needle number fifty or so, I heard
another female screech, and I looked over my
shoulder, and here was Charley Coombs coming to
let the Willoughbys fish by the big rock, and they

have found us. At the time I didn't really stop to think what this intimate tableau must have looked like to anybody coming upon it without previous warning, but as I thought about it afterwards I could see why Mrs. Willoughby screamed. I got to admit it was an unusual moment.

"Well, of course the doctor took right over, and he was just as pleased as could be with the clam-shell tweezers. Couldn't get over what a smart idea they were. Charley Coombs kept his head turned away, being a decent sort, but I stayed right with it, and I couldn't see that a man with a medical degree was any better at pulling out porcupine quills than I was. To make a long story short, we got them all out, and we laid the daughter face down on a canoe thwart, and I paddled her back to camp. The doctor gave her another look-at after he came in, and he said she'd be all right. There were no complications, but that girl sure had a sore tail and some vivid memories.

"What I started to say — this made me an inventor. I got a piece of soft doeskin and some feathers from an old tick up over the guides' camp, and I made a pillow for that girl to sit on. After a few days she came out in the canoe to paint again, and I fixed the little pillow for her and she said it was very comfortable. She sat on it all the rest of the time she was there, and she took it back to Philadelphia with her as a souvenir of her happy vacation in the Maine woods. She said she would keep it always to remember me by. And I'm sure she did. But quite a few people saw the little pillow I'd made for her, and thought my idea was good, so it wasn't very long before everybody on the lake had one like it, and that's how the leather boat cushion came to be invented."

The Bucksaw Ghost

If you want a cord of good dry wood, all fitted, the best place in Maine is the old Marshall Creamer farm in that part of the town of Bowdoin called The Kingdom. They always have wood for sale. A man named Parsons owns the place now, but he's no relation to the Marshall Creamer, who goes back a long time. Nobody lived in The Kingdom then, and Marshall went there as a boy and cleared some land. It was a lonesome place, and after he got a house built he spent some time looking for a girl who would marry him. He'd ask a girl to marry him, but she'd say no, that she wouldn't admire living in The Kingdom. It wasn't long before Marshall had asked every girl around, and they had all refused. But one day Jessie Thurlow said to Marshall, "Marshall, you've asked every girl but me!"

He said, "I ain't?"

"No," she said. "And I've wondered why."

He says, "Why, I would have sworn I had."

She said, "No, you never did, and I'm a little hurt."

"Well," he said. "No offense intended. Purely oversight. Will you marry me?"

"None taken," she answered. "And I will."

So in time there were children on the Creamer farm, and Marshall and Jessie made out first-rate. In all their married life they had only one major point of dissension, and that was the great amount of stovewood Jessie managed to run through her kitchen range. She had never learned how to adjust a damper, and she never would. She would light a fire and then let it roar, most of the heat going up the chimney, and if Marshall undertook to explain about drafts and dampers she would get huffy and say he was picking on her.

Marshall, of course, had to cut the wood, and this gave him some right to be touchy about it. He was handy with an ax and the farm had plenty of trees, but that wasn't the point. So this ran on as a continuing marital friction, and as they both grew older and so got more crotchety, Marshall began putting Jessie on a wood ration. The way this worked, he'd get the wood up every season and stack it in the shed in sled-lengths. Too long for her to get it in the stove. Then, every evening after supper he'd go out to the shed and buck-saw one wheelbarrow load of stovewood. Then he'd push it to the back door and leave it, and that's all the wood Jessie would have for the next day. She could burn it all at once, or she could make it last. It was all one to Marshall. Some evenings when she hadn't been too frugal the house would cool down and they'd have to go to bed to keep warm, but Marshall wouldn't let her begin on the new wheelbarrow load until morning.

What happens when a simple little touchiness like this takes root and grows is common knowledge, and pretty soon the feud was extended into other topics. Jessie would think of something to say to needle Marshall, and then he would needle back, and as they grew older they were fighting all the time — just words, but it was pick, pick, pick. One thing, for instance, was eating between meals. Marshall held that three meals a day and a lunch before bed supplied all normal human needs, and eating between meals was a sin. So one day he found Jessie eating a cookie between dinner and supper, and he took her teeth away from her. He only let her have them at mealtimes. After that they got pickier and pickier.

And one morning about half-past nine he chanced to come into the house, and he found Jessie in the butt'ry gumming some cake, and this was the last straw. He didn't say anything, but he went out and slammed the door. And he never set foot inside the house again. He got some boards and sheathed up a little room over the woodshed, and he got an airtight stove and set it up, and he moved in there and spent the rest of his life. He never spoke to Jessie again, and she never went near him. She ran the house and he ran the farm, and they might as well have been ten miles apart. But every evening after supper Marshall would take down his bucksaw and fit up a wheelbarrow load of wood, and he'd push it to the back door and leave it. Every morning Jessie would come out and lug the wood in the house. It went on and on.

But it couldn't go on forever, and they got over in their books until one night Jessie was asleep in bed and she was brought up by some kind of feeling that came over her. It seemed to her there was a long sigh, as when a tide-turn change of air stirs the popples and balm-o'-Gileads, and it was a kind of sound that bodes no good. It was, of course, the passing of the mortal spirit of Marshall Creamer, and his end had come. He was never seen again, at least in flesh and blood. Jessie naturally didn't go looking for him, but when evening came and there was no wheelbarrow of wood brought to the back door, she suspicioned, and the next day she went over to Bowdoin Center and told her daughter. The daughter came and went up into Marshall's little room, but he wasn't there. He had vanished. The place was tidy and showed no signs of a scuffle. Nobody ever knew and nobody ever found out what happened to Marshall Creamer.

But after three days he came back as a ghost. This is true. Jessie heard the shed door close, and from the kitchen she could hear steps going up the stairs. She looked out, and could see lamplight in the little window over the woodshed. After a time the lamp went out. The next day Jessie went for her daughter again, and another inspection was made of the little room. Nothing. But when evening came, and supper was over, Jessie heard steps on the shed stairway again, and she looked out and saw the ghost of her husband bucking up a wheelbarrow of wood. She even heard the sticks strike the ground when they dropped off. Then she heard the creak of the wheelbarrow wheel, and the load was left at the back door. And in the morning she went out and brought the wood into the kitchen, and that evening the ghost of Marshall Creamer sawed up some more. As long as she lived, Jessie had a wheelbarrow of wood to burn every day. And there was always a light at night in the little upstairs window, and often Jessie would hear that long sigh as of a breeze in the popples.

The real problem came when Jessie died. Nobody knew how to tell the ghost. Even on the night of the wake, the ghost fitted up another wheelbarrow load and wheeled it to the door. They held the funeral, and the ghost never knew a thing about it. During the next few months, with nobody living at the farm, somebody had to come every morning and carry the load into the house, and it got to be a nuisance. By the end of the summer they had twenty-two cords of wood stacked through the rooms. It was at this point that somebody bought the farm.

The fellow who bought it hadn't really meant to locate in The Kingdom, which is still a remote section, but as soon as he heard about the ghost he closed on the spot. He made the family put it in the deed that the ghost goes with the place. He knew a good thing when he saw one.

So the good Yankee ghost of Marshall Creamer continues to buck up a wheelbarrow of wood every evening, and the present owner, Mr. Parsons, is delighted. He remodeled the place and put in some fireplaces. And now and then he sells a little fitted wood. Most ghosts rattle chains and moan in the woodwork, but Marshall Creamer's is a different sort. Mr. Parsons touches up the ax and files the saw now and then, and just last summer he bought the ghost a new wheelbarrow.

Some Foolish Fellows

Before mental retardation was thought up, all Maine communities had a foolish fellow, or half-wit, and there is no limit to the lore they left. A fine example is the story of Bud Hinckley and the time he prevented an Indian massacre. This was on the New Meadows River about the year 1613, and Bud was a slow-witted citizen who provided some amusement in the settlement. There were some few chores he was capable of doing, and one of them was to sit on a vantage point and keep an eye out for marauding Indians, while the menfolks did their work in the field.

(At Fenway Park in Boston the radio booth is located so that a portion of the grandstand obscures the left-field line. Every so often a ball is hit and the left fielder has to run for it, and the radio broadcaster can't see what is taking place. Mel Parnell, one of the broadcasters, always says, "From our vantage point we can't follow the play." This, any semanticist must agree, is an odd kind of vantage point. Bud Hinckley was given one from which he could see.)

Bud would stand on a stump along the edge of the field, and while the men hoed corn he would peer into the surrounding forest, and if he saw an Indian he was to let out a yell and everybody would run for the blockhouse. Other boys, mostly keener than Bud, stood on other stumps in other parts of the field. Standing the boys on stumps was a wise method, because they could be seen by the men, who thus knew they still had a lookout, and as long as the boys were standing up, the men knew they weren't asleep. With Bud, however, you couldn't always be sure, and on this particular day he actually did fall asleep, and continued to stand there as if he hadn't. Then he woke up.

Directly in front of him, on the edge of the forest, was an Indian. The Indian had crawled up while Bud was dozing, and here he was all set to strike. The discovery baffled Bud's slow mind, and he reacted in an odd way. Instead of yelling, he jumped off the stump and ran and stuck his head in a hollow log lying a short distance away — the old ostrich thing. This perplexed the Indian, who saw no reason in it, and in turn it flustered him. It struck him funny.

The men in the field, meantime, had seen none of this, and having heard no yell had not looked up. The Indian, meantime, had clucked like a partridge, or something, and had assembled all the other Indians in the raiding party, and they stood there looking at Bud Hinckley's backside sticking out of the end of the log. Hilarity set in, and suddenly the men working in the field looked up and saw a wild bunch of hysterical Indians dancing around a hollow log. Grabbing up their weapons they started for the

Indians, but when they got close enough to shoot, they were also close enough to see that the occasion was not murderous, but rather, tinged with good humor. Then they could see Bud's backside, and they joined the Indians in a good laugh. Friendship resulted, and having come to massacre, the Indians stayed for supper, and everything turned out fine, and there was a long period of peace. Bud Hinckley saved the settlement.

A great part of this foolish-fellow folklore lingers in a limbo of lost references, because nobody today is a foolish fellow. Emotional imbalance, disturbed personalities, intellectual deficiencies, and similar niceties have taken his place. So, too, janitors have become custodians, paupers have become indigents, and night watchmen have become security officers. Maine has no more half-wits, janitors, paupers, and night watchmen, and if you seek half-wit folklore nobody knows what you're talking about. And another thing — a good part of the half-wit folklore is fragmentary, or boiled down to localisms that make sense only to the people who know the rest of the story. The esoteric values evaporate with lengthy explanations and literary research. As an example, there is one Maine town where two people, meeting on the street, will speak thus:

"Large evening!"

"Great air!"

They meet and pass, having made this exchange, and there is nothing more than that. The foolish fellow who, years ago, inaugurated all this has long

been forgotten, but he spoke these lines to all he met until they became traditional — just as "Yes, we have no bananas!" was made a national byword by daily repetition in a cartoon. In another town the local joke is "It must be the weather!" Hardly anybody in town remembers Chet, who was the halfwit. Chet, long ago, was standing by the post office one afternoon, and the minister's wife passed by. Having no intellectual responsibilities, Chet spoke to her affably, tipped his hat. He said, "Good afternoon, Mrs. Wilbur — how's your backside?"

The indelicacy of this, since some ten or a dozen other men were standing there, gave the lady much embarrassment, but she knew Chet, as did everybody, and she was willing to concede that he wasn't "all there." Patronizingly, she turned to him, and in tones intended to reprimand she said, "Oh, Chet — shut up!"

Chet said, "So's mine — must be the weather!"

Today, in that town, "It must be the weather!" is a localism with solid historic foundation, but only those to the community born will know just what it means.

Another town mildly perpetuates a half-wit's observation that "it must be raining all over." The foolish fellow was around the post office on a rainy morning, and he saw farmers coming in, and no matter what part of town they came from, they said it was raining there. His conclusion that it was raining all over was logical, and was worth remembering. So, if one citizen observes that it is storming, another will answer, "Eyah, it's raining all over."

This is certainly no worse than the traditional Maine-wide dialogue:

"Think it will rain?"

"It always has."

Or the variant: "Be a long, dry spell if it don't."

Or sometimes, when rain is coming down in sheets and somebody says, "Think it'll rain?" the answer is, "Well, I notice it's clouding up."

A good half-wit story is about the two fellows who went out on the pond in a boat to go fishing, and they had such good luck they wanted to mark the place. So one of them put a cross on the side of the boat. The other one said, "That's foolish! What if we don't get the same boat next time?"

Some sections of Maine run to sagas of foolish-fellow stories, sometimes based on true or presumedly run-out families. Amos Tuttle of Wellington is hero of many a yarn. He was a big fellow, and they used to yoke him in with a steer and plow with him. They'd brad him and thump him on the nose, and he'd work just as well as an ox. One day they turned up a bumblebee nest, and Amos and the steer got frightened and ran away. They cornered them in a fence finally, and Amos yelled, "Unyoke the steer first — I'll stand!"

He is said to be the one who drove a horse and buggy down to Skowhegan to see the first steam train come in on the Bingham line, and he thought the horse might take a fright, so he unhitched him and tied him behind the hotel. Then he had to move the buggy so the expressmen could do their work, and while he had the "sharves" in his hands the

train came in, and it frightened Amos and he ran
away and smashed up the buggy.

Amos, and a thousand other Maine half-wits, may
be assigned to the fidding story. In ox days a long
logging chain ran from the yoke to the load, and
according as work was done this chain was sometimes too long. It could be shortened by thrusting
one link through another and inserting a "fid." This
was just an iron pin, or a bolt. One day Amos was
pulling stumps and he shortened up the chain, and
he stuck his thumb in the link for a fid and yelled for
the oxen to take up. A variant is about the horse
teamster who, to leave his hands free, wound the
reins around his neck and then had his animals run
away. He saw his mistake at once, and regretted it.
Stepchild of the fid story is the Paul Bunyan tale of
Babe the blue ox, who was hitched on ahead to
move a load the other oxen couldn't start. When the
chain came taut it lifted the smaller oxen off the
ground, and they strangled in their bows before Babe
could be slacked off. And perhaps another stepchild
is the tale of the man who lost his finger in the sawmill, and a few days later he was showing somebody
how it happened, with the heartrending refrain,
"Migawd, there goes another one!" A seacoast variant might be the man who hove the anchor when the
line was around his ankle, or the man who hove the
anchor when he had no line on it at all. Or of the
lumber schooner that began to leak, and the crew
baled and pumped night and day — keeping her
afloat until they got to Boston. There they found the
whole bottom had dropped off the vessel, but being

loaded with pine boards she wouldn't have sunk, anyway.

And there is one aspect of the foolish-fellow story which merits separate consideration in its own chapter.

The Muscular Mother

Thus, sometimes folklorists permit some halfwit deductions, and get hung up. I shall offer two examples.

One is the authentic folklore story of the pioneer housewife who tossed fish to the wolves during a severe blizzard. A great deal of momentum, and consequently much credence, has been given this tale down through the years by an assortment of folklorists who, if they paused to think, would have kept silent. One expert, indeed, isolated it (it had already been isolated fifteen times) and ascribed it to his own grandmother.

This story goes that this saintly pioneer mother, giving her all to bring up an honest, happy, Christian-oriented family, took her small babe in arms one day and walked down to the "landing" to get some fish. It was about a three-mile walk, more or less. There seems to be no explanation as to just why she did this, for she had many a broad-bottomed son and also a broad-bottomed husband who could have gone and got some fish without taking the baby along. There is also some discrepancy about the fish. In some versions she got alewives, which don't run until after the blizzard season is over, and in some versions she got pogies, which are menhaden and a fish not worth the bringing home and best rendered for paint oil. But this woman was lucky, and when she got to the landing she found some boats had just come in, and there were plenty of alewives, or pogies, for everybody, and she gathered up three quintals of the fish and started home, still carrying her baby.

Then it comes off to snow. Not a common run-of-the-mill storm, but a real, wild, sub-zero blizzard with gale winds, and biting, stinging flakes that cut and burn. It settled in from the no'theast, great swirling blankets of snow that hid the world and made it almost impossible to breathe. Time and again this mother was ready to collapse along the way, and death and oblivion teased her as the pleasant way out. But she struggled along, waist-deep in the drifts, her eyes stinging from the blast, and her cheeks frostbitten. Then the wolves came.

A pack of ferocious, hungry wolves; eyes blazing and their famished fangs poised for the strike. They closed in.

But this brave woman was not a pioneer mother for nothing. Just as the foremost wolf was to sink his tusks in her, she tossed down a fish behind her, and while the wolf pack pounced on the fish, fought over it, and devoured it, the woman pressed on through the storm and gained valuable distance. After the wolves ate the fish they came on again, of course, and then she threw them another fish. All the way home, just as they were to bring her down, she tossed more fish, and at last she came to her own gate and her own door, and she threw the last fish and thus saved herself and her baby from a horrible fate. No doubt she burst into the house and turned to fit the big bar on the door, and her husband and six husky sons looked up from the fireside and asked if anything was amiss. Anyway, the story is extant, may be found in many a compendium, and it has a happy ending.

The half-wit trouble seems to be that nobody ever took the time to ask what a quintal of fish is. A quintal is one hundred pounds. So you can see that folklore breeds big, strong, husky, muscular mothers who can pick up three hundred pounds of fish and a baby and run three miles in a snowstorm ahead of a pack of wolves. This story is frequently told by people who turn around and laugh at Bud Hinckley.

A far more satisfactory version of the same general yarn is the one about Cy Nye. Cy bought a side of beef and picked it up under one arm and started home with it. Something made him meditate, and as he walked along he forgot that he had bought the beef. So he suddenly recalled his errand, and he went back to the store and bought another side. It was kind of comical to see him with two when he only meant to have one, but perhaps Cy could really carry three quintals of alewives.

The second example of this sort of thing is the Hannah Dustin tale, which has become settled as history, rather than folklore. It is nonsense, either way. Many stories persist, like the one with the wolves, to demonstrate the fortitude of the women, and very common is the one where the Indians abducted a wife and started for St. Francis with her — either as a hostage or as a woman. On the trail they camped overnight, and the woman arose in stealth, sunk a hatchet in the head of each Indian, and came back to the settlement safe and sound, bringing the scalps to prove her story. This gory nugget has been accepted without question by generations of scholars and folklore experts.

It has one basic fault which would be recognized only by people who have gone about hitting other people on the head. It is not too quiet an amusement. I recall one time Danny Snow hit a line drive and it sailed into the stands and hit Henry Dalrymple on the forehead. I was playing left field, and Henry was in the first-base stands, and I heard the baseball hit him as distinctly as if it had hit me. He ran about a little, eyes glazed, and they chased him down and gave first aid. He was all right, but I'll never forget the noise it makes when somebody gets hit on the head. Another time I was standing outside the barn, and I heard a magnificent thwock! and I ran into the barn and found my father all fuzzy and bewildered. The cow had swung her head at a fly, and the curve of her horn had caught him just above the ear. He was all right after a few minutes, but again, I'll never forget what it sounds like when a human head is bumped.

Consequently, I have never believed that a woman went about in the dark and bashed in the skulls of sleeping Indians — the first one she crushed would have been an alarm for the others. That she succeeded in killing the Indians is probably doubtless, but how she got them may someday be better explained. However, let us not carp at that — the main point on which this story is hinged is the bringing back of the scalps. Of course she brought back the scalps, but it was not as the historian says, "to prove what she had done." The reason she brought back the scalps was to collect the bounty which was offered by the colonial government. It sounds a trifle degrading in this day and age to admit that our ancestors were so uncouth and forthright. But they were, and if scalping today has never been authentically portrayed in all the Wild West movies we have seen, it was nevertheless practiced in those days. Hannah didn't being back the scalps to prove what she had done; she brought them back so she could collect three pounds, seven shillings and sixpence — which in those days would put a boy through college so he could study folklore.

Why Frankie Was Late

Young Frankie was late for school one morning, and thus begins the remarkable legend of the ailing hog and the heroism pertaining thereto. This story is found in Waldoboro, New Sharon, Solon, Brighton, Bar Mills, Blue Hill, and Ashland. Frankie's father was a farmer of consequence in one of the aforesaid communities, living two and one-half miles from the village. Now since Frankie was late for school this morning, and had walked that distance to come to school, it might seem frivolous of a teacher to make something of it. Furthermore, on the day preceding this tardiness there had been a substantial blizzard, and the fact that Frankie came at all, late or not, was worth noting, as the roads were still drifted. But these were the good old days, and keeping school still had some connection with education, and a boy was expected to embrace heartily the opportunities offered by the taxpayers. The teacher said, "Frankie, you are late!"

Frankie, who was ten years old and still had short legs for Maine snowdrifts, made answer thus: "Yes, ma'am — I was up all night."

Being up all night was not a common practice in those days for anybody, let alone a growing ten-year-old boy, so the teacher was concerned by the thought, and also had some curiosity. Upon asking Frankie the reason for his lack of sleep, she was told, "The hog was sick."

Frankie's father had a blue-ribbon sow that had taken prizes in every fair, and the days were accomplished that she should be delivered. This old sow would sometimes throw fifteen pigs at a whack, and they were as good as gold in the economy of the farm household — bringing a dollar apiece at six weeks. If she did her work, a brood sow was just like money in the bank. And on this evening Frankie's father had gone down to the barn to see how his prize hog was coming along, and he was distraught to observe that she appeared indifferent. Being an old hand at home remedies, he was concerned, and tried to make the old girl comfortable. But almost at once he decided some dire mischance was afoot, and he knew the pig was in bad shape. He tried to give her some warm water, which she wouldn't take, and he rolled her over on some clean straw and covered her with horse blankets. But in the end he knew he was not helping her any, and he came up to the house.

He went up to Frankie's room, where Frankie had gone to bed with a soapstone to listen to the wind ripping dry crystals of snow against his window, and eventually to drop off to sleep. He wakened Frankie, and he said, "Get up, Frankie, you've got to help me! The old sow is sick, and I'm afraid I'm going to lose her. I've got the horse hitched in the pung ready to go, and I want you to ride to the village and get some medicine. Put on your warm clothes and bundle up, because there's a snowstorm."

So Frankie got up and dressed, and when he came down into the kitchen his father told him, "Now, go right into the village, and go to Fred Randall's house. It's the one on the corner across from the post office. You'll have to pound hard on the door to wake him up, but you tell him who you are and that your father's hog seems to have a fever. Don't let him give you no for an answer. You'll have to wait for him to dress, and then you go with him to his drugstore. He'll give you something for the hog, and you bring it home as soon as you can. Now, it's a bad storm, so don't try to trot old Tige. But make him go along steady-like. I don't want to lose that sow and her pigs, so I'm counting on you. All right?"

Frankie said yes, everything was all right, and he got in the pung and started for the village. Old Tige lumbered along through the snow, but he kept going. He knew the road, and Frankie didn't really have to drive him — but it was fierce cold, and snow lashed Frankie's face until he hid it under the blanket and only looked out now and then. When he got to town he did just as his father had told him. He pounded on Fred Randall's door until he came down, and he told Mr. Randall that his father had a sick hog.

"A sick hog!" said Mr. Randall.

"Yes," Frankie said. "It's his prize sow, and she's due to farrer, and he said I wasn't to take no for an answer and to be as quick as I could."

"You drove down in this storm!" said Mr. Randall. "Then I guess I can step across the street!" So he pulled on some clothes, and he and Frankie went to the drugstore, and Mr. Randall lit a lamp out back and began looking at bottles. He would look at a bottle and wag his head and put it back on the shelf. He said, "A sick hog, I dunno — if it was a human I might be some help." Finally he said, "Well, maybe . . ." and he mixed something up in a bottle and gave it to Frankie. "Put this inside your coat where it won't freeze, and I'll go back to bed and pray it works." Frankie climbed back in the pung and went home.

But it was worse now. The snow was well up on Tige's legs, and in some places the drifts made him wallow. But a horse going home is better than one going away, and Tige kept plugging along, and at last they came to the dooryard. Frankie's father was down in the barn with the sow, but he heard the bells on old Tige and he came up to get the medicine. He thanked Frankie and told him to go back to bed because it was almost morning and it would be schooltime before he knew it. Then he mixed the medicine with some warm water in a long-necked whiskey bottle, and he went down and very tenderly coaxed it into the old sow. In abstemious Maine a long-necked whiskey bottle was not as hard to come by as some might think, and it was ideal for getting a dose of medicine into an animal. You held up the snout and let the bottle gurgle down, and you stroked the beast's throat to make him swallow. The sow took the dose, seeming almost grateful, without any fuss. And almost at once she seemed some better, and it appeared that the fever had broken.

After that Frankie's father was too tired to go to bed, so he sat up in the rocking chair until daylight, and when Frankie came down for breakfast his mother was trying to be quiet with everything and Frankie's father was sound asleep. But he woke up soon, and without waiting to eat he went right down to the barn. So what with this and that, and being up all night, as well as the snowstorm, Frankie was late for school. The teacher heard him out and was touched.

"Why, Frankie," she said, "I think that's a very brave thing you did, and we're all just as proud of you as can be. It must give you a wonderful feeling to know that you saved that hog's life on such a wild night!"

"Yes'm," said Frankie. "Except that when Father went down to the barn this morning, the old sow was dead."

Down-East Thrift

When Henry W. Kingsbury, M.D., reached sixty-five he sold his practice and retired. Ever since he had completed the two years of close study at the Maine Medical School he had cared for the folks in the Buckfield, Hartford, and Peru section, and he was a beloved citizen held in the highest esteem by all. No storm ever kept him from coming when he was called, and now that he was leaving them the people gathered in the Grange Hall for a big testimonial supper. They gave him a three-piece Thomas flyrod in token of their love and affection. The doc had a camp up in The Enchanted, and he had said that he planned to spend the summers there and go to Floridy in the winter. He introduced the young man who was taking over his practice, and also made everybody stand and applaud his wife. Mary Kingsbury had stood right beside the doctor all the way, and the whole town loved her as much as they did him. It was a wonderful evening.

So Dr. Kingsbury and Mary took off for The Enchanted, and they had a perfectly wonderful summer fishing and reading. No babies, no broken bones, no snuffy colds, no vaccinations, no midnight calls. They stayed on until the lake began to freeze around the edges, and then they closed the camp and came down

to Buckfield on their way to Florida. Dr. Kingsbury
went in to see how the new doctor was making out.

"Dr. Kingsbury," said the young man, "I can't
figure it out. I put in four years in college, four more
in medical school, two years in a hospital, and two
years in the Army Medical Corps, and I came
here and took over your practice under a complete
and cruel illusion. I thought I'd have a comfortable
backcountry practice where I could make a decent
living, bring my children up in healthy rural surroundings, have my Wednesday afternoons for rabbit-hunting and trout-fishing, and some day retire, as
you have, with a little laid by to make my old age
enjoyable. Well, I've been here all summer, and I
love it. It's a beautiful region, with good, honest
Maine people. But the plain truth is that I can't make
a living here. There just plain isn't that much sick-
ness in Buckfield. Some days I don't have a patient
at all. Last week I had one broken finger, one piece
of emery wheel in one eye, one baby with colic, and
one overdose of steamed clams. I'm starving to death.
But here you are, retired and money in the bank, a
camp in Maine and a house in Florida. How did you
do it?"

Dr. Kingsbury leaned back in the chair and looked
at the young doctor for a full minute. He smiled as if
in recollection, and then in confidential tone he
spoke.

"Dr. Jansen," he said, "I'm going to tell you. It
was State-of-Maine perspicacity and down-east
thrift that made me a successful country practitioner, and my medical education really had very

little to do with it. When I was first out of school I married Mary, and we came up here full of hope and ginger and we thought, just as you did, that we'd have the world by the tail on a downhill cant. We looked forward to a happy life filled to the brim, and we presumed that Buckfield would support us. But we found out just what you found out — this is a healthy place. There were people in these hills ninety years old who never saw the inside of a physician's office. So I had to develop perspicacity.

"What we'd do, Mary and I, was to go for Sunday walks. We'd take a lunch and some baskets and a book on botany, and we'd study the wild flowers and the bushes, and we got so that we knew all about them. The right ones, we'd gather them up and bring them home in the baskets, and we'd hang them to dry in the attic. Then we'd study what we could do with them. Mary would steep them on the stove, and we'd see what they tasted like, and after a while we came up with a secret formula for a tonic. It was pretty good. It had bad taste enough to seem useful, but it was different from anything else. We didn't have anything in it that would hurt anybody, and I guess we didn't have anything that would do them any good. But it was plausible. Mary had the recipe written on the kitchen wall, and so nobody would see it we had a picture of Grace Darling and her father hanging over it. She'd take the picture down and make a batch, and a batch was five gallons.

"Then I went down to Auburn, and I went to the old Dr. True's Elixir factory, and I gave them five dollars for a whole wagon of odd bottles. Some bottles were green and some were red. They threw in cork stoppers for them. And then I went to a printer and got some labels printed — just plain labels that I could write on with a pen so each bottle looked as if it was special for each patient. Except for the bottles and labels we didn't have a cent involved, and I was all ready to put my perspicacity to the test.

"So what I'd do, I'd go to the post office and I'd meet somebody like Martha Hastings, and I'd shake hands with her and make small talk, ask her if her husband was cutting pulp, and finally I'd say, 'Martha, occurs to me you haven't been in lately for a checkup.'

" 'No,' she'd say. 'I been feeling tip-top. No aches nor pains. Didn't see the need.'

" 'Well,' I'd say, 'it don't pay to go overlong. Our age, you know. Sometimes things creep up on you and you don't know it.' That's all I'd have to say. It always worked. They'd get to thinking about it, and it might be a day or it might be a month, but one day they'd come in and I'd get a dollar for an office call — and they'd get a real checkup, which was a sound thing to have anyway. Then I'd say, 'Now, Martha, I don't find a thing to be suspicious about, and I give you a clean bill of health. But age has a way of creeping on, and this is always a bad time of year, so I think I'll prescribe my tonic for a week or so.' So I'd get another dollar for a bottle of my tonic, and I'd tell them to come back after two weeks.

"All right. So after two weeks they'd come back, and I'd ask if they'd noticed any improvement, and sometimes they'd say yes and sometimes they'd say no. It was all one, but I'd take another dollar for that office call, and I'd check their hearts and lungs and pulse, and they always went away feeling better, and it was cheap at any price. But this is where down-east thrift comes in. My perspicacity paid off, but my down-east thrift was yet to come. Just as they were leaving I'd say, 'Oh, one thing I didn't do — I didn't test a urine sample. Would you bring one in next time you happen by?'

"Now, in that way I got my bottles back. . . ."

The Phantom Ship

Sometimes Maine antiquities insinuate themselves into a modern context and astonish the scholars, as well as everybody else. So it was with the Dead Ship of Harpswell, which gained literary security in the verses of the same name by John Greenleaf Whittier. Mr. Whittier was pretty fair on folklore, but his geography was about fifteen miles off. The Dead Ship of Harpswell was from Freeport, across the bay. She was a vessel which may be said to have foundered on fact, and the facts are easy to come by. When the War of 1812 was about to burst into full bloom, the astute and forehanded Porters of Portland contracted to have a ship built at Porter's Landing in Freeport by Master Brewer, and their specifications appear to have been prophetic. The vessel was launched as the *Dash*, and her construction and equipping had been so thoughtfully arranged that she was all ready to go as soon as word came that it was all right for her to do so. She was a pirate. Now, nobody called her a pirate in those days, because when a country goes to war it can quickly think up all manner of nice words for mean things. In this instance the word was "privateer." But the *Dash* was a pirate all the same, and she went looking for British ships in a distinction without much difference, and she was mighty good at it. The Porters were good, honest, upright people, and they made out fine. But after about fifteen sorties the *Dash* set out on another, and something happened, and that was the end of her. Her crew was made up entirely of boys from Freeport, and there was weeping on the hill.

Well, so much for that. Most people thought she probably had her top-heavy chasing sails up, getting ready for fun, when a squall hit her, or she tried to tack in a Fundy tide just at the wrong minute. It could be.

Then one evening, off Punkin Nubb — a small rock island in the mouth of Freeport's harbor — Simon Bibber was jigging for bait pollock. He was out there in a peapod with a cask amidships, and they were coming good. He'd jerk one in and slat it into the cask, and he had it about two-thirds full already with the tide serving, so he'd fill it easy. Just then the weather shifted, and one of those quick fogs so common to Casco Bay settled in. They're a kind of fog that doesn't really come in — but all at once it's there, and you're all alone in a great blank world. The fog didn't bother Simon any, the pollock kept coming and he was just a short pull from home, but the fog is part of the folklore. All at once Simon

heard the creak of lines in sail blocks, and the rush
of water at a prow, and he looked up scarce abaft his
own elbow to see a full-rigged sailing vessel careen
past him, and on through the channel into Freeport
harbor.

Now if Simon had had his wits about him he'd
have thought this was remarkable. When you are
hunkered in with a thick Casco Bay fog of that kind,
you don't have any wind. And this vessel tore past
him as if a gale was rousting her on through. She was
laid over and hull up, and every sail was filled. But
as she went by Simon saw the stern, and he read:
"*Dash* — Freeport." "My gorries," said Simon,
"She's the *Dash*!" So he folds his jig and grabs up
his sweeps, and he pushes for the town landing, because he knows there's going to be some hijinks to-
night with the *Dash* home. Been long months since
everybody thought she was lost. Well, when Simon
came humping up to the town landing he saw some
small craft in the fog, but no big vessels, and there
was no *Dash* anywhere in sight. He found Mort Col-
lins mending pots on the wharf, and he says, "Mort,
what become of the *Dash*?"

Mort says, "The *Dash*! Where the hell you been?
She was lost long ago!"

"No," says Simon. "I seen her. I was pollocking
out at Punkin Nubb, and I seen her come in, all sails
set and all hands on deck."

"With no breeze?" says Mort.

Well, that set Simon to thinking, and for a time
he thought he was losing his mind. He went home
that night and sat in the rocker and looked a long

hour at nothing, and his wife asked him if he was all right. He got ribbed a little for "seeing things," but he kept his peace and didn't press the thing. And along in late August, Roscoe Moulton came up to Simon one day and drew him apart, and very confidentially he said, "Sime, you recall telling how you seen the *Dash*?"

"Eyah."

"Well, I'm kind of cautious about this — but I seen her, too."

"Eyah?"

"Eyah. Down by Crab Island. I was hauling a pot and I near got run down. She flew past me like a whirlwind, and they warn't a breath of air stirring, thick o' fog and a flat-arse calm. I seen her."

Well, after that quite a few "seen" her, but doubts continued to prevail until one afternoon the *Dash* came into Freeport harbor and went right by the *Betty Macomber*, a Banks schooner coming back with cod, and the entire crew of seventeen men all saw the *Dash* at the same time.

"The ghost of what was once a ship is sailing up the Bay," sings John Greenleaf Whittier.

After that nobody had any doubts. She was the *Dash*, all right, and in a good fog-mull she'd come home. Along Whaleboat, Eagle Island, Pound o' Tea, Crab Island. Always laid away over, in calm air, through the thick-o'-fog, she'd sail by, white water at her prow and all the crew on deck looking into the fog toward home.

Which is all right as folklore and poetry, and amusement for the children. But sometimes Maine antiquities have a way of thrusting forward, and the *Dash* did that. During World War II the Navy took over Casco Bay, and they made quite a nuisance of themselves. They drew lines on the charts, and a fellow had to be mighty careful where he sank a pot. You could get over one of these lines and spark a crisis. It wasn't much fun to be a fisherman or try any boating, and they'd shoot at you sometimes if you tried to find a mess of clams. The British Navy took over the back cove at Cumberland Foreside, and one day you'd see it full of destroyers and know that the next day there'd be a convoy strike out. The bay was under what they called tight security, and they warn't just a-kiddin'. Anywhere from Bailey Island to Biddeford Pool they had patrol boats going and coming like herring in a rain bar'l.

So, one August afternoon one of these Casco Bay fogs settles in and you could have looked at your own wife at the end of your nose and not known her from Adam, or Eve either, and when you can't tell Adam from Eve you've got a fog. So all at once the United States Navy radar gong goes off, and everything hikes into action, and sirens blew and tarps came off cannon, and all hands took to stations, and there is a red warning clear back to Buffalo, New York. The defenses were being penetrated, and a blip was coming right into the most restricted zone, and while the infallible system told them everything else, it didn't tell the Navy that the *Dash* was coming home to Freeport again.

Even the British turned out. They came sweeping out of Cumberland Cove biting off the water in great chunks, and shooting as they came. They acted as if Sir Francis Drake was personally in command. The poor *Dash* came up past Eagle Island, Whaleboat, Crab Island, and Pound o'Tea, and they were shooting at her every inch of the way. The United States Marines, in particular, were extremely effective. It was one of the greatest concentrations of power and might in the entire war, including the landing at Okinawa, and this is attested to by a relatively unimportant witness named Homer Grimm. All folklorists will agree that Homer belongs in this story. He, too, operated in the fog.

Homer lived on Staples Point, and when all conditions coincided and there would be a suitable fog, he would row his small skiff across to Wolf's Neck, not a great distance, and he would do this with the general idea that nobody was going to see him. On a clear day Homer avoided Wolf's Neck studiously. The reason was that Homer, when he got to Wolf's Neck in the fog, would touch in at a certain point, and by felicitous prearrangement the voluptuous wife of Googie Bragdon would be there, and she would get in Homer's skiff and he would row out to Punkin Nubb and they'd go ashore. Then after a seemly meanwhile he would row her back to Wolf's Neck, and after that he would go home to Staples Point. In short, the same conditions that suited The Dead Ship of Harpswell were the happiest days of Homer's life. This, then, was one of his happy days.

It would not be kind to make historical record of the precise moment and mood that prevailed when the *Dash* came past Punkin Nubb on this foggy afternoon; suffice to say that Homer and the comely Mrs. Bragdon were both interrupted and astonished. When the projectile from the British warship took the corner off a ledge barely ten feet from their island love nest, they at first assumed that their little secret had been discovered. They naturally supposed that somebody was shooting at them. They peeped cautiously over the rock but could see nothing for the fog, and just then, right in their very faces and eyes, came the *Dash*, ripping through the channel in her customary way — sails crowding and all hands peering ahead at home. Immediately came the Coast Guard, the Navy, and H.M.S. *Moidore*, sirens going, horns blatting, guns blazing. Homer & Co., delighted to realize the attack was not on them, made haste to shorten their tryst, and he began to row her back to Wolf's Neck. Thus it was that they were in mid-channel with the skiff when all the war boats, finding no *Dash* in the harbor, swept back out into the bay in great puzzlement and confusion, and practically every boat stopped and asked Homer if he had chanced to see anything of a sailing vessel. The usual serenity of Homer's pleasant assignation did not prevail that day. It was disturbing, to say the least, to realize that his well-kept secret, when discovered, became an official United States Navy matter.

The Navy, however, hushed everything up. Shore patrols went from house to house all evening asking questions, and after a sufficient number of people offered that it must have been the *Dash*, it was impossible not to pay heed. When the top brass finally had to accept the improbable, namely: that the United

States Navy had attacked a phantom ship, the records became vaporish. It was a thankful situation where Homer wasn't going to mention the Navy, and the Navy wasn't going to mention Homer.

The Last Caribou

The last caribou in Maine was sighted by seventeen different unimpeachable authorities in seventeen different places. Will Andrews, whose story is told here, saw the last caribou at Lily Bay, on Moosehead Lake, in the late fall of 1902. The departure of the caribou from Maine was considered mysterious at the time, but biologists now say it was because of the disappearance of certain foods, this in turn caused by lumbering. The French-Canadian lumberjacks had their own simple way of explaining it. They said, "The car'boo, she's afraid of stumps." This was true; as stumps increased, the caribou's food decreased. The animals didn't fade away or die off, they migrated into Canada — never to return.

Will Andrews told me his story himself:

"It wasn't exactly the last caribou, because it was a herd of fourteen. I had plenty of time to count them. The head of the herd was a magnificent bull with the finest horns I ever saw, and the minute I saw him I wanted his head to mount. It's quite a story.

"Joe Greene and I went partners that fall, and we were trapping around Lily Bay from a camp we had there. We had one line over as far as Kokadjo,

so we were covering quite a territory. Well, one week-
end I walked down to Greenville, not only to see the
family but to pick up some things we needed, and I
skated back. The lake ice was as smooth as glass, and
while it was a cold day there wasn't much wind, and
I went right along. I'll never forget my little dog.
We had a short-haired dog, and he wanted to go
back to Lily Bay with me, but I wouldn't let him.
He was taught to mind, and when I told him he
couldn't come he knew I meant it. But he came down
to the lake with me while I was making ready, and he
took to shivering — the way a short-haired dog will.
He sat there with his tail on the ice and trembled like
a leaf. Never was so cold in his life, but he was going to stay until the last minute, and he did. So I
packed things and clamped my skates onto my boots.
I had a moose sled, what some people call a hand-
shark, and I was taking a canoe back. I put the canoe
on the sled gun'l-up so I could lay things in it, and I
had some blankets and some clothing. I had two pair
snowshoes and some groceries. Nothing that would
freeze. Then I had some books and magazines, and
some tobacco for Joe, and so on. Now, I want to explain about the gun, because that's important. I had
my own .40-65 — a gun you don't see anymore, but
it was common in those days. Great moose gun. But
my ammunition for it was in camp at Lily Bay. But,
I had three boxes of .32-special ammunition I was
taking in for Joe. You see, I had a gun with no
shells, and I had some shells with no gun. Mixed up,
but that's the way it was. Well, I got my skates on,
and I picked up the handle of the sled and I began

to pull. It started hard, but once I got it moving it slid right along and it wasn't any effort. Once I got speed up I just picked them up and laid them down, and the fourteen miles up to Lily Bay wouldn't take as long as you'd think. I was far out when I looked back the last time, and I could still see that dog sitting there. He never made a move to follow me. Well-taught dog.

"All right. So I came to the last point of land before swinging into Lily Bay, and Joe and I had a deadfall for a fisher set just a little way up from the lake, and I decided to check it on the way by, which I did. I left the sled on the ice, took off my skates, and I walked up to the deadfall. I suppose not too many people recall how a deadfall worked. You take a log and trigger it, and when the fisher tackles the bait, the log drops and pins him. Well, I came to the trap and it had been tripped, and I had me a fisher. A good one, too. I took him out and reset the deadfall, and just then I heard a noise all around me, and I looked up, and I was completely surrounded by caribou. Fourteen of them, with this big bull mighty prominent. They weren't alarmed, and they looked me all over and then ran off. But they didn't go any-place, and I could see the herd was just milling around in that spot. So I was put to wondering how I could get that bull, so I could mount his head, and I chuckled to myself realizing that all I had was a .40-65 rifle with .32-special shells. And that was back on the sled on the ice.

"Well, I sneaked down to the sled. I tossed an empty knapsack on, to put the fisher in, first, and then I took my .40-65 and put a .32-special shell in it — wondering if by any chance it would work. I set the shell in very deliberate, to line the pin up, and I cocked the thing and pulled the trigger. It went off. The shell fired all right. Well, you can imagine what happens when a small casing explodes in a big chamber, and that shell was jammed in so I had to use my knife to pry it out. But I got it out, and I carefully fitted in another .32-special — and this time I tried for accuracy. I drew on a piece of moss on a tree, and the gun went off all right, and I hit the moss. So, I headed back up on the knoll to see if I could get a shot at Mr. Caribou. I had the third .32-special laid in, all set to go, and I took good time moving back up so I wouldn't alarm the herd.

"I came back to the deadfall, and I picked up the fisher and put him in my knapsack, and I carefully moved where I thought the caribou would be. But they came to me. All at once I heard this great noise again, and they came charging up together, and they took up a position all around me, just as they had the first time, and here was this big rauncher right ahead of me — not fifty feet away. He was side-on, so I could heart him and not hurt the head a bit. I raised the gun very slowly, not making a single false motion, and I drew a bead right down to a whisper, and I touched her off.

"Well, this time the bullet didn't explode. Never went off. You don't have any idea what kind of a noise a bullet makes when you are aimed at a caribou and nothing fires. It was such a complete and total nothing that I stood there dumbfounded, as if I was in a trance. And just then it appears that this fisher I had put in my knapsack hadn't been dead at all, but was only stunned, and now he comes alive and begins exercising his rights inside my knapsack on my back, and I can guarantee this is the greatest thing in the world for bringing anybody out of a trance. I suppose I'm the only living man who ever had a live fisher in a knapsack on his back while surrounded by caribou. The fisher went around and around like a thunderstorm, and what with the wonderment already upon me over that bullet which didn't fire, I was in a case. It must have been a spectacular exhibition to those caribou. I dropped the rifle, slammed the knapsack on the ground and jumped up and down on it, and while I was doing this the caribou all went away.

"And that's the last time I ever saw a caribou in the State of Maine."

Horse in a Well

This whole thing started with Will Davis. Will had a trout in his well, and one day he looked down and the trout was gone. Somebody had fished it out. Will wondered what kind of low character would do such a thing, so he decided to find out. He never told anybody about losing his trout — not even his own wife. Then, seven years later, Will was in the post office and he got to talking with Sherm Prout, and all at once Sherm says, "Oh, by the way, Will — did you ever find out who caught that trout out of your well?"

Will says, "Yes."

What started it off was that a stranger in the crowd spoke up and said, "A trout in a well? What would anybody have a trout in his well for?"

"All the old folks kept trout in their wells," said Bun Bartley. "A trout's a clean fish, and the idea was it would eat the grasshoppers and crickets that fell in. A trout kept the water pure."

"It did, too," said Flint Johnson. "My old man had a well that used to go flat now and then, and he put a trout in it, and it never went flat again. But it's a funny thing. You can't keep two trout in a well. One of them will always eat the other."

So this stranger said, "I think this is just one of your Maine tall stories. I don't believe anybody ever kept a trout in a well. That's ridiculous!"

Well, of course they fixed him up good before they were done with him. Flint said, "I can strike right out from here, and I guarantee in a day's time I can find you a dozen wells with trout."

This fellow was a writer — forget his name, but he did short stories for the *Saturday Evening Post* — so he leaped at this, and he made Flint prove it. Flint did. He found five wells with trout close by. But then this writer-fellow was going up to Parmachenee Lake, working on a story no doubt, and in those days the Parmachenee Club was run by Curly Hamlin, who used to be game warden. You couldn't drive to the camps, but had to leave your car down to the

Brown Company chain, and then Curly would come out with a station wagon to get you. You'd drive to the chain and park, and then telephone in. So while this writer-fellow was driving up, Flint calls Curly on the telephone and tips him off.

Curly was no hand to neglect an opportunity, so by the time this fellow gets to the chain they have everything set up. They get to the float and Curly is about to paddle the guest over to the camps on the island, and as the fellow is getting into the canoe he notices it has some water in it, and swimming around in the water are some trout.

Curly shows great concern and apologizes. "Damn things is everywhere — cussid nuisance!" And Curly tips the canoe up and pours the water into the lake, trout and all. Then when they get to camp Curly takes the fellow into the dining room for a lunch, and here on the table is a glass water pitcher with a trout in it. After that everything the fellow sees has a trout in it, and the climax comes when he goes in to use the flush bowl and he's got one in that, too.

So it went, but the thing was they pestered this writer with this stuff for years. Any time anybody could think up something, they'd send him a post card. And clippings. Gene Smith had a cow wander, and she fell in a well, and everybody sent newspaper clippings of how the firemen came and got the cow out. They all wrote on it, "Trout isn't the only thing!" Johnny Galgovich was rabbit-hunting one time, and he came onto an abandoned well in the woods, and here was a moose in it. The game wardens came and they had quite a time, but they got the moose out, and everybody sent clippings of that.

But the big payoff was when Lon Ridley teamed a load of logs across his lawn, and the horses broke through some planking and went into a well. Lon didn't know the well was there. But he had a mess on his hands, and the call went out. They got the first horse out right away; they twisted him around and he was able to step up. But the second horse was wedged in. Lon went down and held the horse's head up above water, and everybody brought ropes and pulleys and debated about how to begin. It took a long time, but they got the horse out, and he was in pitiful shape. They laid him out on the barn floor and covered him with blankets, and set some lighted lanterns in under the blankets, but the horse shivered so the barn shook. Never was a colder horse. Lon thought sure he was going to lose him.

But Leon Bard was there, and Leon telephoned to a vet over in the next town, and the vet said to give the horse three ounces of whiskey every hour. He said this would promote circulation and after four-five-six hours the horse should be all right. Now this was a poor thing to tell Leon, because Leon doesn't touch a drop and as far as he was concerned whiskey was something he neither had nor wanted. But Leon is also a great lover of animals, and this horse was in bad shape. Leon wasn't about to let his own personal opinions cause the death of a good horse, so he struck out to find some whiskey.

In those days, in Maine, this was some errand. You

could get whiskey if you knew where to go, but Leon didn't know where to go. Being a teetotaler, he appeared flustered as he pounded on doors up and down the road and asked if they had any whiskey. People thought it was comical to find Leon out looking for booze. Furthermore, in that neighborhood, some discretion prevailed over admitting that you had spirits in the house, and, being a known dry, Leon was not considered a good risk. Besides, whenever he tried to explain that he wanted it for a horse, hilarity prevailed. In desperation Leon finally came to the home of Albert W. Plummer, M.D.

Dr. Plummer was a-bed, but he came to Leon's thump in a bathrobe, and he said, "Well, good evening, Leon — what seems to be the trouble?"

Leon said, "Doc, I need some whiskey."

Dr. Plummer said, "So do I — come on in."

Hearing the tale, Dr. Plummer pointed out that the Maine laws were not broadly enough enacted to cover this precise situation at this hour. Besides, while he could give Leon a drink, he doubted the legality of giving one to a horse. Leon said he didn't want a drink. But after Dr. Plummer milked all the humor out of having Leon come for whiskey, he fixed things up, and Leon got some and headed back to the Ridley farm.

The horse was still shaking, so they quickly made ready to dose him, and they had one awful time of it. That horse was just as much a teetotaler as Leon, and he wasn't about to sully his gullet with the demon rotgut of John Barleycorn. He kicked and squealed and slat his head and chomped, and the men all backed off. But farmers know how to do these things, and they got him trussed, with a strap around his nose, and they got the whiskey into him. He didn't think much of it. But the men noticed that almost at once he breathed easier, and they thought some of the shivering abated. They agreed there was some response.

At the end of the hour they made ready to give the second dose. They got the ropes and straps on, and Leon stood ready to shove the bottle in as soon as the men pried the horse's mouth open.

But everybody was pleased to see the horse didn't struggle so much, and this time it wasn't hard at all.

On the third dose, the horse reached up for it.

Everybody sent clippings about this to the writer-fellow, but he never put any of it in the *Saturday Evening Post*. You can see, though, how stealing a trout from Will Davis's well led to Leon Bard's making a drunkard out of a horse.

The Poor Pooch

The most frequently unpublished story in American literature is an ancient piece of Maine folklore about lobster meat. Harold Trowbridge Pulsifer, the poet who was also a magazine editor, remarked once that its incidence was on a par with the common cold, and it used to be submitted almost every day as if it had just happened somewhere. It came from every point on the globe in a thousand different contexts and versions. When Pulsifer came to Maine to live he heard it again orally all up and down the coast, and he came to the professional and literary opinion that it was valid Maine folklore, on the grounds that it revolved around lobster meat and Maine was the logical source.

Lobsters are a perishable commodity. A lobster who is not bright-eyed and alert when he comes to the kettle is traditionally regarded as a bearer of ptomaine poisoning. But if he is apprehended just before he becomes a "weak" lobster, he may be thrust into boiling water and still be construed as an asset. Picked-out lobster meat, free of shells, thus comes to market. Now, to keep the lobster industry from starting suit for defamation, be it added that such lobster meat, in the aggregate, is just as good as any, and there is no reason to abuse it. However, in the old days before advanced refrigeration, this did not need to be so, and this story is about the old days. Once in a while there might have been some lobster meat which was not good.

And thus it happened that there was a notice in the paper one day, and it said, "The regular Tuesday meeting of the Friday Club will be held on Thursday this week instead of Monday, at the home of Mrs. Bradley Footer, retiring president. Roll call will be quotations from Swinburne, and a guest-night buffet will follow the meeting."

This was to be the usual final fling of the outgoing president. She would preside, install the new officers, and then the husbands would come and they'd all have supper. To prepare for this Mrs. Footer had engaged the Massingale String Quintet from Bangor, which would render Brahms. And she had also engaged Nellie Gleason to come and lend a hand. Nellie was the community's available assistance, and she would arrive at breakfast time on the Thursday and spend the day — dusting, arranging chairs, helping with the kitchen preparations, serving the buffet, and finally cleaning up the dishes. Hardly anybody held an important party without Nellie, and you could practically leave her alone and she'd do everything. So after she finished her coffee she went right to work. She had everything well in hand at once, and Mrs. Footer had nothing to worry about. The members would arrive at two, and while Mrs. Footer was busy with the meeting Nellie would marshal the food and put on the finishing touches. In due time Nellie went to the ice chest, for this was long ago, and brought forth the bowl of lobster meat which was to be made into the salad. Automatically, and with proper Maine reflexes, she rolled a bit of the meat between her thumb and finger, and then she sniffed it. Her expression was uncertain.

"Mrs. Footer!" she said. "Are you sure this lobster meat is fresh?"

"Oh, yes," said Mrs. Footer. "Perfectly fresh. Mr. Footer knows the man who puts it up, and he wouldn't send us anything that wasn't strictly fresh."

"Well, I don't know," said Nellie. "It don't seem to crumble right, and I thought it smelled a mite weak. But I could be wrong."

"No," said Mrs. Footer. "I'm sure it's all right."

"Maybe," said Nellie. "It's your party."

Thus the seeds of doubt were sown, and with lobster meat, doubts don't have to grow too high. "I'm going to give some to the dog," said Nellie.

Here is folklore, sweet and pure. Folklore says a dog won't eat spoiled lobster meat, and if it has the slightest suggestion he'll turn his nose up and walk away. Nellie put a few pieces of lobster meat on a plate and set it down for the dog. The Footer dog sniffed it, gobbled it down, and looked up as good dogs do to see if there would be any more. "That proves it," said Nellie. "The meat's good."

The meeting was entirely successful. The quotations from Swinburne set a happy pace, and the election of officers pleased the nominating committee. Mrs. Footer delivered her retirement oration, and pinned a corsage on each new officer as she took her station. The Massingale String Quintet was delightful, and it played right up to five-thirty, when the first menfolks began to arrive. The collation was delicious.

Nellie had on a white uniform, and she hustled in and out from the kitchen. Mrs. Footer stood by the beautiful buffet table urging everybody to have more, and when they came up to get more they all remarked on how lovely everything was. Some members also congratulated Nellie, because a good part had been her doing, so Nellie was pleased. After dessert and coffee there was some standing around in groups, and Mrs. Footer was wandering from one to the other to permit all to extend appreciated felicitations on the excellence of the occasion, and Nellie was going and coming with dirty dishes, and the party was practically over.

So in comes Nellie from the kitchen, and she sidles up alongside Mrs. Footer so nobody else will hear what she says, because she is the bearer of bad news, and she whispers, "The dog is dead!"

Well now, you just better believe that Mrs. Footer received this news with considerable agitation. But she was a forthright and reliable woman, and duty and obligation were words that meant something to her. There was no hesitation whatever — she stepped right across the room to Dr. Roger Hathaway, who fortunately was present as a member's husband, and she told him quickly the whole story. He, too, was forthright, and he briefly said, "Don't worry one bit, Millicent," and he went to work. He called for attention, explained about the lobster meat, asked everybody to remain calm and as relaxed as possible, and he sent two men to his office to fetch stomach pumps.

It was a dismal ending for such a lovely party. It is said not to be pleasurable to have your stomach pumped out under any circumstances. One by one, everybody's life was saved. Dr. Hathaway, last of all, gave Millicent Footer two little white pills to take, saying she should go to bed at once. And she went out into the kitchen to find a glass of water so she could take the two little pills. Nellie looked up from the sink and said, "I just can't help it — I keep thinking about that poor little dog!"

"Yes," said Mrs. Footer, "but he died a hero. If it hadn't been for him, the whole Friday Club would have died a horrible death!"

Nellie said, "Why, Mrs. Footer — you got it all wrong! The dog got run over by the grocery wagon out in the street!"

About Another Grant

The temptation to include Edward Grant generously in this scholarly study is resisted on the grounds that a good part of him has passed over into formal literature. The story of his pet trout has not only appeared in print, but it has become a standard classic in the world at large. When Harold Pulsifer was named one of the world's seven best sportsmen, because of his agitation for the barbless hook, he attended an awards dinner in Sweden. Harold didn't know any Swedish, so the speeches meant little to him, but while one man was talking Harold kept hearing him say, "Ed Grant" Afterwards Harold found somebody who could interpret, and he learned that this speaker was relating the story of Ed Grant's pet trout. Harold asked if the speaker had known Ed Grant, and he hadn't. Harold asked if the speaker had ever been to Maine, or known about Beaver Pond and Kennebago. He hadn't. But the story had wandered, and most happily Ed Grant's name went along with it — it is seldom "the story of the pet trout"; it is, rather, "the story of Ed Grant's pet trout." In 1904, long after Ed originated the tale, Francis I. Maule of Philadelphia took it down during one of Ed's lengthy narrations and it was printed in a booklet called "The Tame Trout and other Backwoods Fairy Tales as narrated by that Veracious Chronicler, Edward Grant, Esq., of Beaver Pond, Maine." In later years a more pretentious volume depicting Ed Grant as the world's most honest man appeared. So, much of Ed Grant moved from folklore to letters.

Students should, however, remember that the *words* were not the important thing — these Ed Grant tales included the personality and narrative talent of Ed Grant. He sucked on his briar pipe, smoked cords of kitchen matches, and milked everything to the last drop. And he was strictly in the tradition of the one-eyed minstrel who took his lyre down from the peg, because Ed Grant operated in a remote region where the evenings were long and he had small competition for his tales. He was a troubadour in the true sense — sitting before the fire with an appreciative audience that had nothing to do except listen. He ran a hunting-and-fishing camp, where woodland vacations brought him an income. He was a backwoods humorist with a perfect, if natural, talent, theatrical as well as literary. Excepting only Paul Bunyan, he is Maine's richest source.

In his story of the rowing race, the subtlety of his invention is quickly seen. He is asked if he ever pitted his remarkable rowing ability against suitable competition, and he says yes, that there was one time he was challenged to a rowing race by two Harvard students. This, right there, is about as funny as you can get. Two Dartmouth students, two Yale students, two Cornell students — they would have no special comedy context in the Maine woods. But two Harvard students is immediately funny. He had no trouble beating the boys, of course, but he came across the lake so fast that friction on the water set his boat afire, and he had to beach it to save his own life. Indeed, the lake boiled from the heat, and a good many minnows and chubs were cooked.

Around the Rangeley-Kennebago region, Ed Grant is also recalled for witticisms and pleasantries not precisely "stories." As he led guests in over the tedious trail to his camp, he tried to keep them amused, and at one place they would come upon a huge rock the size of a house, and Ed would stop, look at it, waggle his head, and say, "My gorry, how that thing has growed!"

"Yep," he'd say. "When I first came into this country as a boy, that was just a small pebble I shied at a pa'tridge!"

He had the same formula when he came to the place where guests could look off and see Boyle Mountain. "It's much bigger now — when I first saw it, 'twas just a pimple."

Afterwards Ed widened the foot trail into a sort of road, and he had a buckboard and horse to assist guests in and out of his woods. But it wasn't much of a road. He would load the baggage and guests on the buckboard, cluck to the old horse, and after about a hundred yards the guests found out it was far better to walk than ride. The buckboard would arrive at camp with everybody following it on foot.

This led to the very first formal printed advertising any Maine wilderness resort attempted. The following year Ed had the road in a little better condition, and his advertisement in the paper said, "Guests will find the road greatly improved. Hardly anybody has been killed on it this season."

Ed became famous for his ability to guess the weight of a fish. Guests would bring in a catch, lay it on the counter, and Ed would squint at it and tell them how much it was going to weigh. He never missed. One time a couple of guests came in with a "racer" they'd caught at Little Kennebago Pool. A racer is a salmon that failed to spawn, and its biology is affected so the poor thing grows long and lean and it will soon cease and desist. This fish they brought in was about two feet long and about the size of a rake handle. But the two fishermen stopped at the blacksmith shop and pushed about eight pounds of scrap iron down the gullet of this skinny salmon. Then they came in and asked Ed to guess its weight.

Ed squinted, and there was no possible way he could know about the scrap iron. But he was a good judge of humanity, and perhaps from the way the men looked he got an inkling. He squinted some more. "Wa-al," he said, "that's a mighty fine salmon, and I'm going to guess it'll go ten pounds, two and three-quarters ounces."

Well, the fish probably weighed about a pound and a half, but when they put it on the scales the beam went up to ten pounds, two and three-quarters ounces.

Ed said, "That's close enough."

But when Ed Grant had pegged his last cribbage hole, his affairs passed to his son Will, and Will spent a lifetime living up to the traditions handed down, and listening to innumerable people who shook his hand to say, "I knew your father!" Will, in his own way, was equal to all of it. First, the camps at Beaver Pond and then the big set of camps known as Grants, at the outlet of Kennebago Lake, continued to serve a delighted clientele, and Will was never found wanting in his hospitality and entertainment. Two stories will suffice, here, to give Will Grant a niche in Maine folklore on his very own, without reference to the fame of his father.

When the last hunter left in the fall, the Grant family would settle in at Kennebago for the winter. It was really a pleasant life. Ample food, plenty of firewood, and a snowbound world of incomparable beauty. Until the ice went out in May, the Grant family lived by themselves unto themselves. The state sent in a schoolmarm who lived with them. And when stars with tinkly points stood sharp in the sky and the thermometer thudded to forty below, an evening with the Grants was a cozy family affair. Under the deep snow the lake would stretch away for five miles, and now and again the ice would boom and proclaim the cold — but it was warm in the home.

On this one particular night the solid domesticity was complete. Janice and Barbara, the two girls, were at a table with the sweet girl high-school graduate who had taken her first teaching job, and they were working on arithmetic under an oil lamp. Mother Grant, turned in her chair so she could use the same light, was doing some fancywork. Alden, the smallest boy, was puttering with some ice-fishing traps, and the two older boys were working on some skinning boards. Under another lamp, apart, Father Will was having a close cribbage match with Winnie Raymond, the game warden. Winnie had come on snowshoes, making his periodic rounds of his territory, and by custom would cadge free meals and a bed. It was such a pleasant scene, everybody content, and only the occasional boom of the lake ice came to remind them that the Maine winter had struck forty below.

Now, across the lake, in that area known as The Big Sag, there was, at that time, a lumber camp. Engaged in cutting long spruce, the crew of thirty-two men included a French-Canadian cook, a P-I boss, a Bangor clerk, and twenty-nine Polack choppers who couldn't speak a word of French Canadian, P-I, and Bangor. As always, this camp was plagued by bedbugs and in this connection the French-Canadian cook had offered the usual Maine woods cure — kerosene. From time to time kerosene would be applied to the cracks in the logs, and this deterred the pest, at least for a while. It also created a combustible condition, and by some unlucky chance this proved to be the critical evening. Somebody struck a match, and almost instantly a French Canadian, a P-I boss, a Bangor clerk, and twenty-nine Polack choppers were standing in the snow with the weather at forty below, and they were watching their only shelter and all their possessions disappear before their eyes.

It is necessary to explain that the nightgown, or pajama, was unknown in the Maine lumber camp, and that a true woodsman stripped raw when it came time to retire, and wrapped himself in a blanket which was known as a "paper-mill felt," and that because of this interesting custom the thirty-two men now standing in the snow were naked. Three and one-half miles away, across the frozen lake, they could see the faint yellow gleam of a window at Grants, and as this was their nearest help, aid, and assistance, they began to dogtrot, single file, in that direction.

This is why, with the Grant family quietly absorbed in their own pleasant activities, their door unexpectedly burst open and thirty-two naked men came in out of the cold. It was, as the son Alden told me years later, a great surprise. Mother Grant hustled the two girls and the schoolmarm into a bedroom, told them to toss out all the blankets they could, and the emergency was quickly met with no permanent harm to anybody except the lumber camp and the bedbugs. But it goes to show that you don't have to be an Ed Grant to come up with interesting situations.

The other story also involved Winnie Raymond. No sporting camp ever neglected to give good care to a warden, and throughout all of Maine's history the wardens have been grateful. The situation of the Beaver Pond camps points this up. It was thirteen miles over the trail to Canada, and with Maine constitutionally dry this was a distinct asset to Grants. A man could trot up over the trail and bring back a

packsack of Old Smuggler and King's Choice and not only make a day's pay, but assuage the thirsts of guests until they thought there was no other place so fine as Grants. Not only that, but when ice cream came up from the city it came packed with chipped ice and salt. In those days it came on Wednesdays, and the great wooden tubs had to be returned, along with the steel containers, to the ice-cream factory. When all the ice had melted in the tubs, the salt water had to be dumped out, and at Grants it was always dumped in a certain place just beyond the woodshed and on the edge of the forest. There was, of course, no great thought given to this, but it was soon observed that on a pleasant morning you could look out past the woodshed and see as many as two dozen deer pawing the ground and lapping at the salt. This was considered fortuitous. Hunters seldom had to leave without a deer. Futhermore, while the legal season was definite, venison is just as tasty at other times, and Will Grant always had a deer hanging in the icehouse, the same way he tried to keep a little money in the bank. The game warden, in this instance Winnie, scrupulously kept away from the icehouse. Thus it was.

But on a certain day of the week, one August, Winnie showed up at Beaver Pond and seemed sadly preoccupied. Will greeted him enthusiastically and said, "Step in, I have some King's Choice that just happened down."

"No, thanks," Winnie said.

"What's the matter — you sick?"

"No," Winnie said. "I'm all right, but I'm here on a sad errand. I'd rather somebody would beat me up, Will, but they ain't nothing I can do about it."

"Do about what?"

"Well, I got a complaint, and you know how it is when some citizen complains — I don't have no choice."

"Oh!" said Will.

"I got a complaint that you got two deer hanging in your icehouse."

"That's not true," said Will. "I got three — I took another one this morning."

"Well, much as I hate to do it, I got to take you in. If I don't take you in they'll have my badge."

"That's all right," said Will. "You got your duty to do, and I been caught fair and square. No hard feelings, and I sure hope you don't fret any about it. Now, can I buy you a drink?"

"No," said Winnie. "I don't feel this is a drinking occasion. How about Wednesday afternoon at Stratton court?"

"Fine," said Will. "I'll be there — two o'clock all right?"

So, on the following Wednesday, Will Grant rose to a lovely day. The sun hadn't yet come over the hills, but birds were singing in every tree and the lake was smooth as a schoolmarm's leg, with little wispy patches of thin fog rising. Will always looked up first thing every day to admire his world — because it didn't cost him a cent and he had what everybody else spent good money to enjoy.

Will hung his knapsack on his shoulders and

struck out on the trail through Langtown to Stratton. It was still early, and he swung along making good time, and he thought to himself that he was indebted to the law for giving him this pleasant walk through the Maine woods. Peace and quiet. He got down around Tim Pond when he looked up ahead and saw some people coming. Three men.

One was Winnie Raymond. Another was Warden Supervisor Aaron Meade, from Kingfield. And the third was the Honorable Justice Rufus Townshend, himself.

"Good morning, Will," said Judge Townshend with great affability. "We was hoping to get to camp before you started out."

"Yes," said Warden Supervisor Meade. "We felt it was asking quite a lot to have you come clear'n into Stratton this way, so we thought we'd come and hold court where it was more convenient for you."

"I got my framed charter," said the judge, "and we can hold court anywhere in the county I hang it up."

Well, they didn't fool Will one bit. The last thing anybody in Maine law and justice would want to do was offend an honest, upright camp owner just thirteen miles from Canada. The constabulary and the judiciary, in Maine, have never been that foolish. Will wasn't about to be beguiled. So he said:

"This is decent of you gentlemen, and don't think I'm not grateful. I don't know of anything that's happened in years that I appreciated so much. But the truth is, no matter how warm our bonds of personal friendship, that I been caught in an illegal act, and I'm guilty all the way. I'm an honest citizen and willing to take my medicine. I wouldn't feel right if courtesies were extended to me that didn't prevail with everybody else. So I've been ordered to appear in court in Stratton, and I don't think we should do it any other way. Now if you'll just turn around and walk with me, we'll go out and hold court."

This upset any plans the trio had about Old Smuggler and King's Choice, but they saw nothing else to do, so they held court that afternoon in Stratton.

Winnie said, "I hate to say this, and I could just bite my tongue off, but it's true — I found three deer hanging in Will's icehouse."

"That's right," said Will. "I waive the formalities — I plead guilty."

"Winnie don't feel a bit worse about this than I do," said Judge Townshend, "but like him I got no choice. I have to impose a fine of two hundred dollars, but I know the wardens will agree that we can waive the costs."

"I appreciate that," said Will, "that's very decent," and he counted out two hundred dollars on the desk.

"No hard feelings?" said the judge.

"None whatever," said Will. "And to prove it, I'm going to take a room at Arnold Trail Inn, and in my pack I just happen to have two quarts of very fine Canadian whiskey, and if you'd care to stop by a little later I would like to pour you a little something for old time's sake."

In the poker game that took place that evening in Arnold Trail Inn, Will Grant won four hundred and eighty-five dollars.

One time, long ago, Will Grant showed me one of

his most treasured possessions. It was a thirty-eight-page, hand-written letter he had received from a friend — tediously penned by lamplight and complaining about everything. It was signed, "Yours in haste ..."

The Evils of Drink

In a state where taking a drink has ever been illegal and sinful, it is small wonder the stories about imbibing point morals, and serve to discourage illicit traffic and consumption. Consider, for instance, how intoxication ruined the career of Luther Wile and left him the pitiful victim of his own intemperate habits. Luther guided, and until now his had been a routine existence, day to day, depending on the chance customers who came and asked for his services. Go out on the lake, row a boat all day, and come in at night.

But now opportunity thumped loudly on his lintel, and Luther was offered a chance to get into the real money, and to guide with a new and romantic glamor. He was asked if he would guide a party of girl campers two weeks on a canoe trip down the river. This was more like it, and it demanded more planning than Luther usually gave his work. He had to select and approve a half-dozen canoes, assemble the wangan, and lay the time out so there would be a good camping site each evening. And what was hardest for Luther, he had to keep niceties and decorum in mind, for these city young ladies were not accustomed to the rough language and severe conditions that Luther knew all about. And he also decided, rightly, that he would doff the weather-worn old guide's clothing that had served so well all these years, and he would acquire a new wardrobe as befits the head guide on a safari of comely young women. He got a whole new outfit, and it was magnificent.

He had Lincoln green pants and jacket, with a new shirt in shepherd's weave. He had new hi-cut boots. His new hat was rakish, on the Australian slant, and around its brim he had fashioned a circle of lamb's wool into which he had snagged a dozen or so of the most garish flies he could find. They were pretty loud — the kind you use for show instead of fishing. He even had a maribou, which would not be very good on the river. Then he had a new pack basket, of the Micmac style, with a bright green cloth to tie about the opening, and on its back was a handsome leather scabbard holding a sharp new ax. The handle of this ax was virgin hickory, had never felt the caress of a palm in labor, and was smooth, white, and clean, and it stuck up above the band of feathers on his hat about a foot and a half. He also had a new skinning knife, the Canadian kind, with a curved handle and blade; as it swung from his belt it looked colorful and dashing, if not too much like Luther. In such accouterment, thus, did Luther appear to head off into the wilderness with the gay band of camp girls, and he was quite a sight.

By rare misfortune, the evening before the trip was to commence, the guide's camp became a den of iniquity, and what with cards and intoxicating beverages it was a scene of shocking bad taste. Carousing and betting, and since Luther was always mindful of his social obligations and did not want to appear stuck-up, he only refused the once, and then he laid to. Terrible as it sounds, he got smashed. In due time they laid him on his bunk, pack basket and all, and the night passed and morning came. The orient sun sent his cheerful beam o'er the East Range, and everybody got up and went about his business — except Luther, who slept on. At length, however, he stirred and suddenly realized that this was the memorable day on which he was to begin his new opportunity, and that among guides he was now the chosen one and would soon be happily wending down the river with the girls. Consequently he regrouped himself, and pack basket and all, he rose from his bunk and set out.

He strode from the guide's camp as if he walked on eggs, crossed the lawn by the main lobby, went past the dining-room windows, down over the long open space to the lake, and out onto the pier. Every step was measured and precise, and he looked as if John Philip Sousa was playing all the way. "The Stars and Stripes Forever." Luther was a majestic figure in his new rig, with feathers flying and the ax handle sticking straight up, and he kept on going with that same deliberate tread, and he went the length of the pier without faltering, and without faltering he walked right off into the lake.

There was, then, a moment which certainly was not so long as it seemed to the people in the dining room, who saw this. As Luther descended, the ax handle was the final vision, and after this aforementioned moment the ax handle reappeared. It came up as straight and bright as it went down, and everybody was relieved to see that Luther was still attached to it. The lamb's wool now drooped wet feathers down over the brim of his hat, and his hat drooped over his ears. He climbed onto the pier, and then methodically marched back up to the guide's camp, where he crawled into his bunk and remained for three days. Somebody else was hunted up to take the girls down the river, and Luther returned to his former routine of going out in the morning and coming back in the evening and rowing a boat all day. Thus the evil of drink is clearly delineated.

In this same connection, there is the story of how Bucky went down the lake to cheer up his sick friend, Amos Pitcher. Amos had the summer complaint, and he was cooped up in his camp over a week, so Bucky took some steaks and went down to see if he could make him forget his trouble. Along with the steaks and the other ingredients of a hearty supper, Bucky had thoughtfully included a fifth of Old McTavish. He yanked the struggle-string on his outboard, and off he went to call on Amos.

Amos was glad to see him. He related the details of his indisposition, and, as the time had approached, Bucky began deploying his groceries and making ready for supper. He extricated the fifth of Old McTavish carefully, and as he did so a great horror struck him — he had forgotten to bring any ginger ale. "Migod," he said, "I forgot to bring any ginger ale!" The thought of subjecting Old McTavish to the

injustice of ginger ale may bother some people, but for the purposes of this narrative it need only be said that Bucky never took anything except in ginger ale.

So Bucky ran down to the float and he yanked the string on his motor, and he throttled back up the lake to get some ginger ale, and in hardly more than twenty minutes he was back with an adequate supply.

When he walked into Amos's camp with the ginger ale, he found Amos insensible in the woodbox, and the bottle of Old McTavish sitting empty on the table. He never spoke to Amos again. Bucky always said, "Liquor is a curse, and has spoiled many a friendship — especially mine." It is a lesson worth heeding.

Another lesson is found in the weighted pack basket of Dennis Holbrook, who had been addicted to drink but suddenly reformed. Every time he went to town he would come home loaded, and his wife spoke to him severely about this evil habit. She would meet him at the little float down in front of their camp, tie up the boat, and then help him out and into the house and to bed. She was a good hand to hound, and after many years of it Dennis came to the conclusion, all by himself, that she was absolutely right. He decided to surprise her, and he never touched a drop the next time he went to town. All the boys offered him a snort, but he resisted. There was some pleasant banter about this, but Dennis staved it off and he started home as sober as a baby. He had all his supplies in three pack baskets in the boat.

Two of these baskets were full. He had the heavy things in them. But the third basket had a couple of pairs of socks he'd bought, a package of marshmallows, a new sweatshirt for his wife, and a few odds and ends — nothing heavy. But Dennis didn't know that while he was coming and going with his supplies, the boys had sneaked down and put a cement block in his light basket. Dennis didn't know this as he started up the motor and headed for his own camp far down the lake.

Expecting Dennis to be soused as usual, his wife heard the motor coming, and she brought a lantern down to the float to help him ashore and to start the usual upbraiding. But Dennis brought the boat up in a neat swing, and he seemed so proud at this sober feat that his wife became leery of the situation. He certainly did seem agile beyond the customary, and his wife was touched with some slight remorse as she sized things up and realized she had been all ready to accuse him again, and without cause. Dennis said, "I decided to surprise you, and I'm home sober!"

He hefted one of the full pack baskets out of the boat and up onto the dock so nimbly that it certainly proved his assertion, and his wife was pleased. Then he hefted the other full basket up, and this was something he hadn't done so handily in years. "I'm proud of you," said his wife. Then Dennis reached for the third basket, and he applied only the amount of leverage he would need for some socks, marshmallows, and so on, and when that cement block exerted its inertia Dennis was so off balance that he flung himself overboard. When he came up his wife hit him with an oar.

The moral is that when you give up drink, you don't want to have any friends with cement blocks.

Classical Unity

Early rising is a Maine custom. It's called "getting up before breakfast." Lobstermen traditionally rise and depart before dawn; farmers always do their chores before their bacon and eggs. In the woods, the log bunkhouses deep under snow are awake and busy before daylight. Going to bed as soon as "it gets dark under the table" makes it easier to rise in good season. Many a Maine hired man swears he is the hero of the yarn about the farmer who started things off bright and early. This hired man came to work, and the farmer showed him to a splendid room where he went to sleep. In the dark hours before daylight the farmer thumped on his door and shouted, "Get up! Get up! You gonna sleep all day?"

One of the Blackstone boys in Pownal told how he was keeping eighteen milking cows, and he had to get up real early to get them taken care of before breakfast. "But now," he said, "I've got rid of all but six cows, and I lay a-bed to four-thirty."

Another standard is the bucksaw tale. A hired man had been up since "before breakfast," and after supper the farmer suggested he sit up to the kitchen table with the family and pick over dry beans. This is a tedious and uninteresting job, and it goes on and on. Very late, the family decided to go to bed, and the hired man said, "Where do you keep your bucksaw?"

The farmer said, "What do you want a bucksaw for?"

"Well," he said, "It's such a short time to morning around here, I thought it would hardly pay to go to bed, and I'd saw a little until breakfast."

The same theme is found in the observation of the little French Canadian who spent the night in the horse hovel. He was on the trail, and when night came he went into this abandoned camp stable and curled up in his bedroll. It happened that several parties of hunters were moving about, and the little French Canadian had just got settled when in came four hunters. They made quite a stir, and after a time settled down in their bedrolls, but just then along came four more hunters. Still another four came when the second four had quieted. And about that time the first four got up and began making breakfast. Patiently, the little French Canadian endured all this commotion, and as he took off down the trail he said, "It don't take long to spend a night in that place!"

Linneus Colby arose promptly every morning at four-thirty and baked off a pan of cream-tartar biskits for breakfast. He never missed. Every morning. But one morning he overslept, and he didn't wake up until five o'clock. You have no idea how that one little half hour can throw a Maine man's day off, and Linneus never did catch up. After a while he looked up at the clock and he said, "My Lord! Eight-thirty already! Where *has* the forenoon gone!"

Variations on this might amuse the professors: A mowing-machine salesman called on Thaddeus Tupper at seven A.M., and when he rapped on the door Mrs. Tupper came out and said, "Yes?" He said, "I wonder if I could see Mr. Tupper?"

She looked all about, and she said, "Well, I don't know where he is just now — he's been around the dooryard the better part of the forenoon, but he must have gone off . . ."

Or the fellow who came at eight o'clock to see Farmer Brown, and Mrs. Brown said, "Oh, you've got to come early to catch him — he's hitched up and long gone."

The next morning the fellow came at seven, and she said, "No, he's hitched up and long gone." The next morning he came at six, and the next morning he came at five. This time the wife said, "You just missed him — he hung around a good part of the forenoon waiting for you."

When it comes to that early-morning moment, Maine folklore has contributed an interesting literary nicety that has been underrated by the scholars much too long. This has to do with that brisk moment in a lumber camp when the choppers go to breakfast, and with the classical unities of narration. In studying formal literature, the student early comes to the unities of time, place, and action. A single theme in one place at one time. The original close definitions of Aristotle, who remains our best authority on the drama, were eased off a little in later times, so that a "single place" could be a whole city, or a "single time" could be an entire day instead of merely the precise duration of the play itself. The imposition of this discipline was not without effect, and through the centuries gave us many masterpieces.

Now, leaving the unities for a moment, let us consider the early-morning routine in a Maine lumber camp. Long before daylight the cookshack would be astir, and soon thereafter the men would be up. There was certain work to be done before breakfast — the hostlers would have the animals fed, and if the log-hauls were to be iced, that crew would have been out. We are approaching, however, the serving of breakfast. An old log cookshack and dining room had certain rules, and here the cook was the only boss. Even the owner or boss of the camp deferred to the cook in the cook's province. There was no conversation at meals — men were there to eat. Tables were long, with benches, and one could ask for butter, syrup, potatoes — but this was the extent of speaking. It was the law, and a good one, because it kept the peace. When the hour came for the meal, the bull cook or the cookee sounded the "come-and-get-it." This might have been a sophisticated triangle such as western ranches like to effect, but it was more likely a worn-out 54-inch circular saw which, suspended by the arbor hole, would give off more clang than a Paul Revere bell. A peen hammer made a good clapper. Upon the sounding of the come-and-get-it, the men came and got it.

As you can imagine, these were rough and ready men. You didn't cut logs all day on toast and marmalade, and a lumber-camp breakfast was a monumental foundation for a day of hard work on the mountains in below-zero air. And, as you can imagine, these fellows didn't hang back any when they heard the lovely strains of the come-and-get-it. No symphony orchestra ever played as sweet music as the cookee got when he hit a saw blade with a *marteau*. No wild stampede in Wyoming ever out-ran the surge into the dining hall. The elapsed time between the sounding of the gong and the seating of the men was a merest tick. There was no "After you, Alfonse . . ."

Maine's best folklorist is Holman Day, who until a late hour was not included in *The Oxford Companion to American Literature*. His several novels, his numerous books of true Maine folklore verse, his distinguished career as an early motion-picture scenarist, and his years as a Boston journalist, have had no particular recognition. His home, in Auburn, Maine, is inscribed not with his name, but that of a later owner, Dr. Garcelon, who has been dead for years but still announces his office hours on a dilapidated shingle. Yet if all his other accomplishments are ignored, Holman Day deserves a wide niche in the gallery of immortals for his supreme achievement with the classical unities of Aristotle. Nobody in the whole realm of letters ever succeeded in narrowing time, place, and action down to such a literary minimum.

In one of Holman Day's novels, the entire story

takes place between the time the gong is sounded and the men sit down to eat breakfast.

You've got to get up early in the morning to beat that.

History and Folklore

Nobody looks into Maine affairs very far before he is struck with a great truth — that here is the place to make that big distinction between fact and fiction, between history and nonsense. Maine history is given no attention whatever out in the vast nation, yet children in schools are taught all manner of absurdities. Any frothy myth will gain credence from any writer of histories, and year after year in every schoolroom in America they go all out to perpetuate the utter fabrication that Columbus discovered America. Not once in all the years the Pilgrims have been welcomed to Plymouth by the hand-shaking Squanto has any history teacher ever bothered to tell her little pupils that Squanto came from the State of Maine. Instead, the little pupils are led to believe that Squanto was some kind of Massachusetts oddity, and his knowledge of English was a mystery.

It was Parson Weems who had George Washington chop down a cherry tree, and you can't blame Maine for that — but it was Maine's own poet, Henry Wadsworth Longfellow, who thought up the gay little fairy tale of Miles Standish sending to beg Priscilla's hand. "I am a maker of war, not a maker of phrases!" he says in dactylic hexameter, a meter no sane poet would attempt in English, and off goes Johnnie Alden to fetch the message. *The Courtship of Miles Standish* is a lot of bosh. Priscilla Mullen, or Mullein, was a French Huguenot, and the reason Standish couldn't converse with her was that he couldn't talk French. John Alden could. Nor was a Frenchman, or Frenchwoman, any great oddity — Maine was practically overrun with them for a hundred years before the Pilgrims came to Plymouth.

Around 1550 a Frenchman named André Thevet got the whimsical idea he would like to see what North America was like. He wasn't an explorer, but a schoolmaster. He just wanted to take a trip. History teachers may be amazed that he didn't pawn any jewels or seek royal aid — he came over here by the extremely forthright device of going down to the waterfront and buying a ticket. When he got back to France he wrote a book about his trip, which historians continued to ignore. In it he tells about cruising the Penobscot Bay and coming to the place "where the French formerly had a fort." The French word *autrefois* has a fairly definite meaning — not "recently," but "formerly." In other times. If, in the middle of the sixteenth century, a Frenchman uses the word *autrefois* for a fort on the Penobscot River, how close to the magic date of 1492 is he striking?

The story of Squanto raises a similar question. In 1604, sixteen years before the landing at Plymouth, Squanto and other Indians were kidnapped by

George Weymouth and carried to England for exhibition. Thus, Squanto was no freak out of the Massachusetts puckerbrush, but he was a good Maine Indian — sachem of the Pemaquids. Montgomery, the alleged historian, says, "Squanto was the only one left of the tribe that had once lived at Plymouth." Of course, no Indian was ever so stupid he'd live at Plymouth, so that's the way it goes. But when Weymouth brought these Indians to England, where they spent the winter, the proprietors of the trading company involved didn't think Weymouth had done exactly right by the poor savages, so orders were issued that they should be returned to Maine the next spring. As with Thevet and his voyage, we find that boats going to America were a dime a dozen, and you begin to get a little different idea of what was going on. By the time the Pilgrims came, well over one hundred British vessels were loading fish each season at Fisherman's Island, in the Damariscoves, alone. It was, if you recall, to the Damariscoves that the Pilgrims came in 1602, looking for food. They got it, and any notion advanced by the historians that the Pilgrims were alone in a strange, uninhabited New World, is sheer balderdash. When the European fishing fleet returned each spring, the Pilgrims could look out and see sails, and they must have thought the Marblehead Yacht Club was holding a regatta.

In 1613, seven years before Plymouth, a British gunboat came up from Jamestown, Virginia, and although England and France were officially at peace, the limeys saw no reason to hang back, and they opened fire on the French fishing village at Somesville, on Mount Desert Island. The effect of this was to end the French influence in this region — after that the French operated out of Port Royal, Nova Scotia. So, when Priscilla came to Plymouth, Maine was able to send an Indian down from Pemaquid to talk English with Elder Brewster, but we couldn't have any Frenchmen to go courting Priscilla. The first Thanksgiving was not held at Plymouth — it was held at Popham Beach, Maine, in 1607, by the settlers, out of gratitude for their safe voyage to America, and the Rev. Richard Seymour, the chaplain of the settlement, called it a feast and service of thanksgiving.

Since Squanto and his companions had made quite a hit in England in 1604–1605, being introduced to royalty and honored at many a gay party and reception, the historians have no authority to presume that his appearance at Plymouth was a great surprise. The probable truth is that when the Pilgrims were going aboard the *Mayflower* at Plymouth, somebody on the dock said to Elder Brewster, "And if you see Squanto, remember me to him!" An Indian who had been to England would naturally be interested in the arrival in his country of any Englishmen, and as soon as somebody said, "Oh, Squanto, I hear the Pilgrims have finally arrived!" Squanto most naturally hotfooted it over to see if they were anybody he knew. The Pilgrims, seeing him come out of the woods, must have known who he was before he ever opened his head.

The greatest historical myth in American history

is the treason of Benedict Arnold. Not that he didn't defect, but that his defection minimized the true story until he is the most despised man in our schoolbooks. If historians would honestly assess his expedition in 1775 through the Maine wilderness, he might regain some of the gratitude due him — and George Washington wouldn't look quite so tall. We shudder at the grim winter George Washington spent at Valley Forge, and not a soul gives a shiver for Benedict Arnold's men trudging over the Height of Land at Coburn Gore — a physical ordeal that must have made Valley Forge seem like sunbathing in Yucatan. Everybody knows how Washington crossed the Delaware, but not a living schoolboy can describe how Benedict Arnold and his men negotiated Chain of Ponds. Their records say the soldiers' boats "shipped some water." They sure did, and nobody stood up in the boat to have his picture taken.

And nobody even tries to understand the frustration and despondency that sat upon Benedict Arnold when, after his heroic and incredible military leadership, he stood on the shore looking over at the citadel of Quebec and realized what George Washington had done to him. If a man ever needed a friend, it was at that moment.

In 1628, two years before Boston was founded and eight years after Plymouth Rock, the Maine coastal fishing village of Pemaquid had a population of eight hundred — it was the largest settlement in the New World and even bigger than Quebec City. Fish from the Grand Banks, George's Banks, and the Gulf of Maine had been a staple commodity in European markets for centuries, and Maine had a good many people who laughed heartily in 1492 at the good news that Columbus had discovered America. If you pick up the standard boy's biography of Columbus — the one you did a book report on when you were in school — and stop believing folklore for a few minutes, you'll find in the very first chapter a disturbing, and unnoticed, revelation. It says that when rather young, Columbus sailed as cabin boy on a voyage to the British Isles.

There is nothing remarkable in this — the ancient Phoenicians came to Cornwall to trade in tin. But if we weren't so brainwashed with the Columbus myth we'd know what this means. It means, for one thing, that anybody around tidewater in those days knew that you didn't fall off when you came to the end of the earth. It means that if Columbus drew himself up to his historical importance and said, "I believe the earth is round!" somebody would have said, "Yes, and hens lay eggs." If Columbus, when he was in the British Isles, said to some Irish fisherman, "I believe I can sail west and come to the East Indies!" he'd have got the royal ha-ha — any Irish fishermen could have told him it can't be done. There's a big continent in the way. They could tell him all about it; they'd been there. They could show him the charts. The charts their grandfathers had used when they went.

When the Pilgrims decided they would like to move on to the New World, they asked permission to do so from the trading company that had the privileges in Maine. This trading company wasn't much interested in freedom to worship God, and the intangibles of the Pilgrim philosophy. They were in the fish business, and they had a great need for strong and willing workmen who could cut cod and strew salt. So the request was turned down, on the grounds that the Pilgrims were a bunch of dissenters and they would be a disturbing element in the well-ordered society of early Maine. But the Pilgrims kept coming back, and finally the boss man, Sir Ferdinand Gorges, said, "Look, I have nothing against you as Pilgrims, and no doubt you are fine, well-meaning people. But I'm not in the piety business, and I don't want the responsibility of having you around underfoot when we've got work to do. Now, if you want to go over there and carve out a destiny, that's all right with me — but keep south of the Piscataqua River; New Hampshire or Massachusetts would be fine."

In other words, we could have had the Pilgrims in Maine, but we didn't want them.

But Gorges did send word to his fishery stations in Maine that the Pilgrims were on their way, and suggested it might be nice to keep an eye on them. That's why, in 1602, when the Pilgrims came up to the Damariscoves, everybody sort of expected they'd be showing up.

Yet the historian, dealing strictly in folklore, tells us the Pilgrims went ashore at Provincetown to do their laundry, and since this was on a Monday,

"Monday has been washday in New England ever since." Has any folklorist or any historian — or any schoolmarm — ever paused at this titbit of nonsense and reflected on how violently dirty the Pilgrims must have been? Think about one hundred and two passengers, crowded into that tiny *Mayflower* for sixty-six tedious days, with no sanitation facilities.

Pious as they were, they'd have done that washing on a Sunday, if Sunday it were. And how would New England like Sunday for washday? Let us simply wish that folklore and history might be more separately pursued.

A Short Discussion

The indelicacies of sex, and allied topics, have a place in Maine folklore, but to keep an otherwise proper study unsullied they will not be dealt with here at great length. Perhaps we can consider several smallish examples, and then conclude with the tale of Dick Mawhinney and the two Harvard men.

Such as the Beal Island fisherman who took his wife to the doctor, and after an examination the doctor said, "Your wife is pregnant." "Wouldn't wonder," said the fisherman, "she's had every opportunity."

In another, Matthew Spulick, eighty-four, asked if he could have the afternoon off from his work at the

Bickford sawmill. Bickford said, "Why would you want the afternoon off?"

"I want to go to my grandfather's wedding."

"Your grandfather's wedding! F'Gawdsake, how old is your grandfather?"

"He's one hundred and eight."

"Aw, come on, now — what would a man one hundred and eight years old want to get married for?"

"Oh, he don't want to — he's got to!"

Youth and longevity vie with each other in these Maine tales, as when the two small boys on the wharf at Vinalhaven are talking. "How old are you?" said one of them.

"I dunno, how old are you?"

"I'm five."

"Then I must be five, too — I'm as big as you are."

"Well, let's put it like this — do the girls bother you any?"

"Nope."

"Then you're four."

And in Franklin County, not long ago, there was a revival of an old tale when the state welfare inspector refused to grant old-age funds to Nathan Blethen of Temple, even though he was ninety-two, on the grounds that his mother and father were still living and he was not without support. The investigation did reveal, however, that his mother was qualified for aid, and she was given a pregnancy stipend.

A great variety of unwed-mother stories prevail, always related to some poor local girl whose friendliness has become a tradition. One girl, when the doctor leaned over and asked for the name of the father, said, "I didn't catch his name." Another girl had a redheaded baby, and somebody asked if the father was redheaded, and she said, "Why, I don't know — he didn't take his hat off."

Perhaps the commonest, heard all over the state, is the one about the unwed mother who applied to the town selectmen for assistance. She had nine children, and the town official asked, "Now, are these children all by the same father?"

She said, "Well, I don't really know, but I think the twins are."

A perennial Maine nugget, often told with a harelipped or tongue-tied effect, concerns the door-to-door salesman for Jewel Brand tea, who had been out all day driving the backcountry with a horse and wagon, and hadn't sold a pound. Late in the afternoon, weary and discouraged, he decided to try one more house, and he drove up to a big home on a hill overlooking a lake. The woman came at his knock and said, "Yes?"

"Madam," he said in his sales monologue, "I am selling Jewel Brand tea; it's a fine tea, one of the best on the market, and at this time, as a special inducement, I am giving away, absolutely free, with every pound of Jewel Brand tea, one tin urinal!"

"Well," said the woman. "I'm interested. I run a summer boardinghouse here, and sometimes my guest count goes up as high as thirty-five. If I buy thirty-five pounds of Jewel Brand tea, will you give me thirty-five tin urinals?"

Overwhelmed at this sudden burst of prosperity, the young man said, "Madam, if you will buy thirty-five pounds of Jewel Brand tea, I'll build you a mahogany backhouse!"

Also to be considered, as authentic Maine off-color folklore, is the oldie about the boy who said he wasn't going to marry a certain girl because she was uncouth. She heard that he had said this, and the next time he called to take her out she upbraided him. She said, "What the hell gives with all this 'uncouth' crap?"

But all Mainers dearly love the story of Dick Mawhinney and the two Harvard men who came up to go fishing. Dick did some guiding, so he took these two fellows in a canoe up the Machias River, and he gave them a good time, with plenty of fish. During the trip the two Harvard men felt the urge, and asked Dick to set them ashore, which he did. They modestly withdrew far up in the bushes, and while they were gone Dick performed the same duty right out in the open, by the canoe.

When they came back they rummaged in their little bags and brought out soap and towels, and properly washed their hands — something which Dick did not trouble to do.

"Didn't you go to college?" said one of them.

Dick said, "Yes, I have a degree from Bowdoin."

"Well," said the Harvard man, "didn't they teach

you at Bowdoin to wash your hands after you'd been to the bathroom?"

"No, they didn't," said Dick. "At Bowdoin they teach us not to go on our hands."

Home from Sea

The story of the sailor who was going to carry an oar inland until somebody asked him what it was, is as old as the Homeric legends. The Maine version starts out, "Over in Vermont they got an anchor in the town park; it seems a sailor from Matinicus decided one day . . ." The everlasting difference between tidewater and highlands is a big part of Maine life; it must have been fun to see that sailor from Matinicus struggling up through the White Mountains with an anchor when he could just as well have satisfied the folklore with a light ash oar.

A common story in Maine is about the man who undertook to move a boat from a lake down to the ocean, and the great laughter this generated among those who watched. In the old versions he got the boat on a hayrack; in the more modern telling he used a truck and flatbed trailer. Leon Bard, who is supposed to have done it, says, "You don't have to know anything to be a mover in the State of Maine. You just show up to do a job, and you are surrounded by experts; everybody can tell you how to do it." This is what happened to Leon when he went up to Rangeley Lake to get the boat and bring it down to Cundy's Harbor. Everybody in Rangeley stood around and told him just how to load the boat. Then they all laughed, because he'd never get it unloaded. Couldn't do it. The way a boat is made, and the way this one was cradled, the thing would crack down the middle the minute he tried to move it. It was so hilarious to contemplate this predicament that a dozen good Rangeley citizens came down to see the fun as Leon tried to unload this boat. The point being that freshwater people don't know too much about tides — Leon just backed his trailer onto the beach and left it, and when the tide came in it floated his boat off gently, and all the people from Rangeley went home.

The same point is involved in the Hollywood filming of Ruth Moore's novel *Candlemas Bay*. They called it *Deep Waters* when it got to be a movie, and they sent a big camera crew from California to make the fishing pictures at Vinalhaven. The first day they got everything set up just as they wanted it, and the man said, "All right — break for lunch. Everybody back at one-thirty to shoot!" When they came back at one-thirty the tide had gone out, and everything they were going to shoot was ten feet out of sight.

Zabedas Carter was not a ship captain, and probably the only Carter who never was. He came from Carter's Corner in the town of Bowdoin, which gave so many master mariners to the old days of sail that 'twas said everybody in Liverpool thought Carter's Corner was America's principal city. But Zabedas was a carpenter, and he sailed the world around, just as the other Carters did, except he never took out his ticket. If the ship lost a spar at sea he would repair it, but lacking anything else to do, he made ditty boxes and did scrimshaw, and read. And somewhere along the line Zabedas got interested in religion. Not spiritually, but intellectually. He was a heathen, a pagan, an atheist, and anything else you want to call him, and he didn't have a pious bone in his body. His idea of nothing at all was to worship God, and there probably never lived a more complete agnostic and freethinker.

But he got interested in religion. When his ship touched at some strange place he would go ashore and inquire into the principal religion. He would attend services, call on the priest, and so on, and in particular he picked up books about religions. And at sea he would read these books and meditate on the wide variety of man's religions. Indeed, he easily became the world's leading authority on the subject, and from sheer Voodoo to Transcendentalism, from Shinto Temple to the Vatican, he understood each and every sect and schism and could discuss it learnedly — although without any personal preference one to the other.

Now, back at Carter's Corner the parents of Zabedas continued to live in the old family home, and grew old. Zabedas came home rarely, and only between voyages, but he was kind toward his parents, and because he never married, this was his only home. He sent money to pay the taxes, and other money, and now and then some trinket or bauble from a far place to please the old folks. And every once in a while he would ship home a box of books about religion.

As he sailed about, picking up various books and tracts on the subject, he would accumulate volumes until his little carpenter's cabin and shop needed the space, so he would make a chest and pack the books up. These chests were beautiful things, with dovetail, hand carving and inlay, but at the time they were just simple sea chests such as carpenters made to cheat the tedium of a long voyage. When one of these chests laden with books on religion arrived back at the farm in Bowdoin Center, the parents of Zabedas would have it carried up in the shed chamber and stored away, and in time the shed chamber was full of sea chests full of books on religion.

After the parents of Zabedas died, he kept the place up. He paid the taxes, and had an arrangement with somebody to scythe out the dooryard and keep an eye on the shingles, and eventually Zabedas quit the sea and came back to the place to live out his days.

Being a carpenter, he quickly repaired loose boards in the porch, and so on, and shortly he had the place painted and tidy, and among other things, he shelved off the front parlor and made it into a library, where he soon arranged all the books stored in the shed chamber. He had a big leather chair where he could sit and pursue his hobby, and hardly a day went by that the mail didn't bring him another book — for he had standing orders with many a bookstore in a far place to be on the watch for this and that.

All right, so at that time the prevailing theology at Carter's Corner was a Free Will Baptist society which was not only struggling with the problems of salvation, but with the problems of survival — for donations were small and the costs considerable. To this church, one fine Sunday morning soon after he returned home, wended Zabedas Carter — not that he sought the solace and comfort of God's presence, but that he was curious about the way his neighbors worshipped. A goodly turnout inspired the minister to his best, the organ music was delightful, and the choir did a fine job. Zabedas found the whole program interesting, and because he was well situated financially he made a substantial contribution. At the front of the church, after services, Zabedas stepped up to the young minister and thrust out a hand warmly. "Hell of a fine sermon, Parson," he said with enthusiasm.

The minister winced a mite, but let it pass, and he welcomed Zabedas home and expressed his delight that his presence would enhance the congregation. They stood awhile and talked. And it so happened that at one point Zabedas said, "No, Reverend — actually you've got it all wrong, begging your pardon, but the cleavage of Free Will is more subtle than that. Tell you what — I've got the discussion of divine foreknowledge by the Catholic bishop Bossuet at the house, and I'll get it to you. You'll find it helpful, and mighty interesting. It kind of points up the Council of Trent."

Well!

You just didn't, but Zabedas had. He came to

church every Sunday, and every Sunday he would pick, pick, pick at the minister. Even his usual plentiful contribution didn't soften things, and as soon as he could arrange a "call," the young minister got out of Carter's Corner and moved on to a church where his sermons didn't get torn apart. But with the new minister it was just the same. Zabedas came, and he pleasantly and without emotion offered his great knowledge of theology. He would patiently explain how the minister had misunderstood a remark of St. Paul's, the fault lying not in the immediate application, but in a faulty translation during the third century. At Easter he volunteered a few books that traced pagan customs through the Hebrew to the Passover. And so on. Then that minister would move on. The Carter's Corner church couldn't keep a minister above six months. It was no fun preaching to a congregation that included the world's greatest authority on spiritual matters.

When Zabedas came to the end of his own mortal book he left his fortune, and it was considerable, to several colleges and schools, and gave a good hunk to the Carter's Corner Free Will Baptist Church. He also left the church his library. Alas, the money was frittered away in furnaces, fonts, and frills. Alas, the library was soon disposed of as unwanted — it had papacy and paganism and all manner of odd and heathen things, and upon mature reflection the good parson of the time and his supporting deacons fancied it a bad thing to have around. Thus the story of Zabedas Carter comes to an end.

The story of the little slave girl is a forlorn, wispy tale of mariners' coming home — perhaps with overtones a hundred years before its time. You'll find the story around Lubec, Columbia Falls, Cutler, and Machias — far down-east.

The old sea captain and his wife lived in the big house on the hill — a house with a widow's walk and a view toward Spain. It was the usual Maine situation — he had gone to sea as a fuzzy-lipped boy, and after a few astute voyages had accumulated some money. He had the shipwrights timber him a house, and he took his bride. Then he sailed away, and over the years he would come home at intervals of two to three years. His wife never went with him, and they never had any children. The twilight of their lives was descending upon them, and this was a great sadness — they had wanted children, and the big house should have had children. It was approaching the time when the captain would retire from the sea, and truthfully, he hated to come home to a childless old age with no prospect of grandchildren to sail the toy boats he would make, or to hear the tales of pirates off Madagascar.

On his last voyage he was in an African port, and he was taking on a load of slaves for Savannah. These were huge black men from some cannibal tribe in the interior, and they should fetch a fine price, with excellent commissions, in America. The captain stood on the deck watching the cargo come aboard and go below. Among the slaves was a small girl-child, and she clung to one great brute of a buck who was putting up a bit of a tussle as they got him aboard. The girl, of course, couldn't go. She was perhaps four or five, and as the sailors pulled her away from, presumably, her father and pushed her back on shore, the old sea captain's heart was touched, and he stood there all weepy-eyed to think that he had never had a daughter. The thought came to him in an instant, and he brought this little black girl home to Maine with him, to be raised up in the big house on the hill. The story goes that his wife was delighted, and although some few smallish remarks were made about town, the little waif was soon accepted by all, and she became the only daughter they'd ever have.

Well, she grew up to be quite a young lady — did well in school, took piano lessons, and a great love abounded 'twixt the girl and her foster parents, and she assuaged completely the great sadness that had lain upon them at the lack of a child. Now they had a child, and all was serene. Until, sorrowful to relate, the young lady fell ill about the time she was going on seventeen.

Nobody ever really knew her trouble. She became listless, and languished, and although specialists were brought all the way from Boston, nobody could really say what ailed the poor thing. Oh, she recovered afterwards, but for a year or more she lay in bed, and the old captain and his wife were convinced they were going to lose her. Some days she would just lie back on the pillow, staring at nothing, and seemed not to hear anything that was said to her. But now and then she would turn her eyes as if searching, and the captain and his wife would lean close to speak to her and whisper encouragement. The doctors all said that the problem, now, was to get the young lady to eat. They felt that strength to her body would restore her spirits, and that in time she would respond and improve.

But appetite simply wasn't there. Whatever appealing dainty the good wife prepared would get tasted, and perhaps sparingly eaten, but nothing seemed to stir the girl to show interest. Thus it was that one day when she showed some small interest in her surroundings, if not her food, the old sea captain leaned over and begged her to eat. He whispered of his love, and how his old heart wanted to see her strong and well again, and that she must eat to bring this about. "Isn't there something," he said, "that will appeal to you, can't you think of something you'd like to eat?"

"Just name it," he said with tears brimming his eyes, "and we'll bring it — oh, we do so want to see you strong again!"

So the young lady seemed to lapse into the stream of memory, and to the sea captain she seemed to be thinking of all the things she had ever eaten in all her whole life, and one by one she was comparing them to decide just what had been her favorite meal. It took some time, and then the captain seemed to notice a faint twinkle in her eyes, a bit of expression that hadn't been there in months. She even turned her face on the pillow to look up at him. "Yes,

Daddy," she said, and her first words in a long time were a joyful thing to hear. "Yes, Daddy, there is something I'd like. I'd like to have a roasted leg from a baby."

Hey, nonny, nonny.

The Ring of the Ax

Lumbering, in all its folklore, is strictly Maine. Out in Minnesota they have a statue to Paul Bunyan, but every Wisconsin, Minnesota, Oregon, and Washington tale about this lumbering giant came out of Maine and was ages old before any of those states heard the ring of an ax. And back in Maine, all the Paul Bunyan stories were legends before the giant legend of Paul was pieced together like a quilt. Such as the time he sank the British Navy. As a baby, back in his native East Machias, his size created problems for his parents, and an ordinary bedroom cradle was nothing he could use. So a floating cradle was made for him, and each evening he was tucked in so the tide would gently roll his bed and waft him pleasantly to sleep. But one night he was fitful, and he threshed around somewhat in his sleep, and set up a commotion that created great swells in the sea. This swamped the British Navy, which was at anchor nearby, and has never ceased — thus the great Fundy tides are explained.

But farther back, there is the tale of Phineas Gilbert, who dug clams on the New Meadows flats, and stepped down to the water to wash them. He "rocked" them in the tide, using the kind of Maine clam basket which is still called a rocker, and long before Paul Bunyan he set up a commotion which swamped four English frigates at anchor in The Basin. The Basin is there today, a snug harbor where the frigates would have been safe from any storm.

Thanks to collectors of Paul Bunyan tales, and to writers like Holman Day and Stewart Holbrook, the student can research all this with no more expense than the cost of a library card. Long before there were permanent settlements in the New World, the forests of Maine were being exploited. On the Piscataqua River (a name whose Latinity is often mistaken for Indian by enthusiastic summer folks) there was a "Pipestave Landing," in very early times, where ships loaded barrel materials for European coopers. The very earliest log mark, in Maine, was the broad arrow of the King — soon to be followed by private marks by the dozens. These were clearly the folklore forerunner of western branding marks, and for every rustling story off the Great Plains there was an earlier version along the Maine rivers.

Symbolic of all this, perhaps, is the story of the antique ax, handed down father-to-son for generations, and still in use at the family chopping block. True, it had four new heads and seven new handles in all that time, but it was the selfsame ax. Thus Paul Bunyan shows up in Oregon with his old ax.

"I always used three axes when I was chopping. Yes, sir — that way I could be using one while the other two cooled in the brook. Funny thing, I was chopping along Dearing Brook one time and out

comes a game warden. Seems people down the valley
had seen dead fish floating along and told him about
it. It was my hot axes — all innocent-like I was
cooling them in the brook, and they het up the water
and boiled those fish. Oddest thing I ever see. Lucky
he came by in the forenoon; otherwise we'd never
have known. Well, I never chopped after dinner. It
wasn't safe. I'd start about half-past six and whale
into it, and with three axes I could put up four or
five cords of beech and maple. But along about half-
past eleven the chips would begin to come down, and
it was dangerous to be around, so I'd quit for the
day."

It was a peavey that Paul Bunyan dragged on the
ground behind him, one day when he was out for a
walk, and that scratched out the Grand Canyon.
Like Stillson, Graham, Watt, Pullman, and Diesel,
Joseph Peavey of Brewer, Maine, gave his name to
our language until we spell it with a small *p*. Two
common lumbering tools were the pickpole and the
cant hook. Peavey, who dealt in such things, com-
bined the two into one useful implement — he made
a cant hook with a steel pike in the end of it, and he
called it the peavey. It is a tool that doesn't lend itself too well to being picked up and carried, as
would an ax or a saw. Instead, a timberjack will
hold it by the handle and let the steel end drag behind him on the ground. Knowing how a lumber-
man would hold a peavey easily explains the Grand
Canyon.

The peavey was used for rolling, or canting, logs.
The sharp steel "dog" bit into the bark, and by lift-

ing on the handle a man could roll a log by the simple application of leverage. Sometimes it worked in reverse: a man would have a "holt" on a log and its sheer weight would backfire on him, and if he didn't have sense enough to let go he'd get catapulted into the river. But with expert touch this happened seldom enough to make it funny when it did happen. The peavey gave Mainers a wonderful expression, lost on anybody who doesn't know how a peavey works. Since rolling logs downhill is easier than uphill, anybody having a streak of good luck, or finding a job to his liking, is said to "have the world by the tail on a downhill cant."

The double-bitted ax is another Maine refinement, and in a recent television production of *Heidi* it played a major role in good Hollywood manner. At one point in this musical adaptation of the childhood classic, the old Alpine grandfather is shown splitting a little stovewood. There is some reason to doubt that a Snow & Neally double-bitted ax was ever standard in the Swiss Alps, particularly before Snow & Neally invented it, but there it was. Now, axes are made in various patterns and are classified as wedge, half-wedge, and quarter-wedge. The best ax for splitting wood is one which has considerable wedge to it. The double-bitted ax was strictly a chopping ax, with the least wedge to it. No Mainer would seriously attempt to split firewood in such manner as the Alpine grandfather, in Hollywood, was tackling the job. With great force he swung the double-bitted ax over his head and brought it down into the side of a chunk of wood. The only possible result of this energy would be to sink the blade into the wood so it would take ten minutes to get it out for the next whack. Evidently this is just what happened, because for the rest of that scene the camera adroitly shifted focus and direction, and carefully avoided any close shots of the job. Seemingly, they would come in tight on the downswing, and then wait for the actor to get his ax out, after which they would film another downswing. It made a very gay picture.

Worse than that, however, is the way the world handles "skid row." Every city has a seamy section, where derelicts drink canned heat, and so on, and this has become skid row. It was never skid row — it was "skid road." In the Maine woods, long before dawn, a watering crew would be out in the sub-zero weather to ice the road. In the earliest days, oxen and horses would team the great sleds of logs toward the mill, or toward the "brow" by the river. Later, great steam-driven "Lombards" would pull whole trains of sleds. The Lombard tractor first used cleated tracks, and thus was the prototype of the World War I "tanks" and of the whole caterpillar brigade — they were made by the Lombard family in Maine specifically for hauling logs. Icing the roads — or "log hauls" — served an obvious purpose, and one of the coldest and meanest jobs man ever performed was to turn out and sprinkle water before it froze in the tank, before daylight.

With horses and oxen, teaming on these iced roadways had its moments. On any downgrade where the load might run ahead onto the beasts a snub-line was used as a holdback. A hook went into a clevis on the rear of the sled, and the rope from it was wound around a stump at the top of the hill. Just as a longshoreman feeds a hawser off a winch, the snub-line expert would ease off as the load descended. And when, as it sometimes did, the snub-line parted, or if the expert let things get away from him, a teamster would have a wild ride down the skid road. Many a man died with his horses in a tangle of lumber, but if by skill with the reins a driver managed to survive such a ride, he had something to brag about the rest of his life. He was a fellow who knew what skid road meant. Skid row, of course, means nothing.

All the lore of the Maine woods moved west, and a considerable number of Maine woodsmen moved it. Paul himself, tugging his peavey and teaming his blue ox, went along. The cry of "Timber-r-r!" on Puget Sound had a down-east twang to it. But if the thing has the ring of an ax to it, somebody in Maine told it first.

The One-Man Army

In a part of Maine once known as New Boston, and now called West Gray, the first settler was William Goff — a man whose story has often been recut and remodeled and may now be considered a true Maine legend. In 1775 he was already elderly, for he had been a mature citizen in 1745 and had gone with Bill Pepperell to take Louisburg, on Cape Breton Island, from the French. In 1758 he returned to Louisburg with the Boscawen forces, and had gone on for the exercises at Quebec City. He returned to Boston through Maine, and liked the looks of the place, so shortly he came up to carve himself out a farm, and he called the place New Boston.

New Boston was remote, and when the Adamses and Hancocks began stirring things up for the Revolution, Bill Goff didn't hear too much about it. Besides, Bill had a good record as a loyal British soldier, and had acquired his land in Maine because of that. There is no reason to picture him as Revolutionary material — indeed, over his mantel he cherished as a keepsake and souvenir the flintlock he had fired on the Plains of Abraham. It was called a queen's arm, an official British weapon, and it would fetch a pretty penny today from any collector. So while great stir was making up in his old home town of Boston, Bill Goff was unaware of it in New Boston, and when the weather got on the downhill side of March, in 1775, he was busy putting in his wood for the next winter. All good Maine men have always tried to get next winter's wood under cover by Easter. Since Easter is an elusive date, based on ecclesiastical astronomy, this is easier some years than it is others. When Easter comes late there isn't such a sweat. Five weeks' sledding in March was a great boon if the snow held out and the mud hung off, and in the old days had a lot to do with meeting the Easter deadline on firewood.

(Lorenzo W. Weeks, the proprietor of Weeks' Furniture Store and Funeral Parlor in Acton, took advantage of a warm March day, one time, and harnessed his horse into a patent-leather cutter and took his family for a ride. That would be Mr. and Mrs. Weeks and their three small daughters. Somebody, of course, said, "Ah! Five Weeks sledding in March!")

So William Goff of New Boston was putting in his wood. He had a wheelbarrow, and he would fill it at the pile and then push it into the shed, where he would tier the sticks neatly. There is little in this world so beautiful as a neat woodpile. Bill had maybe a cord or so more to take in, and was well ahead of Easter, and as he was trundling the empty wheelbarrow back to the pile he heard somebody call his name, and he looked up to see a man coming. He was Tim Blake, a friend of many years and a colleague at Louisburg. Tim was on his way up to Barton's Mills to buy furs, and had swung over through New Boston to make a social call. They shook, and Bill Goff left his wheelbarrow right where it was, and they went into the house. They had a merry time with food and drink, and recollections of other days, and in the course of the occasion Tim told all about the excitement around Boston. Redcoats everywhere and the harbor full of warships, and rebellion in the air. The militia was ready to respond, and a good many thought it wouldn't be a great while. Stuff to fight with was being piled up handy. Take Lexington and Concord, for instance, and if the English didn't get to those powder kegs before long there might be a hot supper. And so on.

Bill Goff was astonished at all this. He had no notion anything had been cooking. It seemed unlikely

such animosity for the Crown would have developed
in so few years — but then, he'd been away quite a
spell. As he thought about it, he felt his loyalist side
evaporating. People three thousand miles away from
a king certainly wouldn't get mad at a king for no
reason. He found himself getting all upset. Before
long he was mad as a hornet to think of soldiers
and warships coming to Boston to make trouble for
hardworking folks. He wouldn't like it if a redcoat
showed up to order him around. The more he
thought, the madder he got, and being now a first-
rate Maine man, he decided it was high time he did
something about it. The next morning he struck out
for Boston.

The wheelbarrow stood there, where Bill had left
it, halfway between the shed and the pile, until the
American Revolution was over. Bill Goff never finished his wood before that Easter.

He walked to Boston, which would be swifter
than hunting for a sloop at Falmouth. He left home
all fired up, carrying his queen's arm, and went down
to South Gray, where he paused at the home of
widowed Mabel Morse. She had a bullet mold, and
Bill stayed long enough to run off what balls he'd
need to fight a war. He stopped again at a store near
West Falmouth, where he got a supply of powder.
Then he was off, and he ticked away the long miles
to Boston, getting madder at the King with every
step.

The Boston folklore of that spring of 1775 is well
admired by the authorities, and is taught as gospel
in all our costliest schools. That valiant Bostonian,

Paul La Rivière, clapped himself on his *cheval* so swift, and with hurrying hoofbeats set off to warn the Middlesex countryfolk to be up and to arm. Thus the great straightforward bulk of honest history withered and folklore grew like the gourd. The march on Concord was not a comic-opera kind of playful outing, but was a logical military movement for which both sides had prepared thoughtfully. The folklorish Minutemen were not just a bunch of manure-spreading farmers who rose bravely to an occasion, but were a well-trained militia, well organized and led by capable officers who knew their business. The British were regular army, and by no standards a bunch of clowns who got taken in by some lucky country bumpkins. Even Bill Goff, who now approached just as the exercises got under way, was a trained soldier with battle experience. He passed through Medford to Menotomy, and came upon the British retreat. Having his gun, balls, and powder, and a cooperating disposition, he dropped behind a stump and he drew a bead on an English soldier, and he touched off the old queen's arm.

Those things fired when a flint-steel spark touched off the powder in the flashpan, and they spoke with authority. They also made a cloud of powder smoke that immediately obscured the target and would hang around over the countryside for weeks. Bill rolled over two-three times so he could see under this cloud, and he said, "Got him!" Reloading these weapons took about as long as a Supreme Court decision, but Bill reloaded and after a time fired again and said, "Got him!" again. Thus, in hot pursuit of the redcoats, he proceeded, and was doing fine.

But the educational illusion that the Patriots were merely hepped-up locals, ramming around out of extemporaneous ire, must be quieted by the arrival, now, of their officer on horseback, who was keeping an eye on things and telling his men when to head in and when to pull out. He came wheeling up, and all at once he saw this elderly joker taking part, pumping reeking lead, and he did a double take because this wasn't one of his men.

"Hey, there," he yelled. "Who are you and what company are you with?"

Now comes the greatest single remark of the entire American Revolution — putting Ben Franklin and Tom Jefferson to shame, and summing up the entire substance of the American national dream.

Bill rolled over on the ground so he could look up at the officer on his horse, and he shouted, "I ain't with no company! I'm old Bill Goff from up in Maine, and I'm fighting alone!"

There was a Bill Goff of New Boston, and he did walk to Boston to fight the American Revolution all by himself. But this officer on the horse, after the day's excitement died down, came back to find Bill, and signed him up for the duration. Bill lost his individuality in the great democracy of the army, and this was good, because in after years he got a pension.

Well, he came back to New Boston, and in those days there was a Foster family living at Gray Cor-

ners. Mr. Foster had a sister-in-law. This girl's father had been six years of age when Bill Goff marched away to Boston, in 1775. He grew up and married, and his daughter reached courting age when the leaves of autumn were searing on the aged shoulders of Bill Goff. Bill married her, and evidently not because he had to. She was soon a widow, and still a young woman, for Bill presently wrapped the draperies of his couch around him and lay down to eternal dreams.

Bill's child-bride, of course, drew a widow's pension from the United States Government as long as she lived — which was a long, long time.

But Bill came home from the wars, and finished wheeling in his wood, and there is matter there which folklorists have found interesting. The historian, no doubt, will want to go to the archives of the Pentagon, where the pension records are on microfilm and the date of Mrs. Goff's death may be authenticated.

New Boots on the Long Trail

Walking to Boston from Maine was commonplace and by no means invented in Colonial times. Twice, the powers in Washington have officially established a route that the Paint People used a thousand years ago — once when Postmaster General Benjamin Franklin laid out his post roads and set milestones, and again when President Eisenhower defined Interstate 95. In late years there has been some academic interest in establishing the pre-

cise route of Maine's old "Long Trail," but Franklin
and Eisenhower came as close as anybody. It was the
coastal route, originally a walking trail that also
made use of bodies of water, and canoes. In some
places today parts of it may be seen and easily recognized, but in other places conjecture is necessary.
But we do know there was such a route, and there
are historical references to it.

During the American Revolution, George Washington sent some lieutenants to get a little manpower
from the Micmac Indians in New Brunswick. We are
taught in school that King George III was a mean
old thing because he hired Hessian soldiers, merce-
naries, to come over here and fight his battles. Evidently, schoolteachers think a war is no good unless
you do it yourself. But nothing is offered about pious
old George Washington's doing the same mean thing,
so we don't hear too much about these Micmacs. The
lieutenants coursed the old Long Trail, and in pow-
wow convinced the Micmac braves that they would
be well paid if they came down to Boston to fight.
Several hundred warriors thus started down the
Long Trail, headed for Boston. But soon after they
started out, one of the Indians wised up, and he suggested they leave the Long Trail and finish the trip
by water. So a courier was sent on ahead, being able
to cover the distance alone much faster than the
group, and the Micmacs showed Washington's lieutenants how to strike south and come to the ocean —
which they did at Machias. The courier had done his
work, and a vessel arrived. So the rest of the long
walk to Boston was a boat ride — but reference to

the Long Trail is noted. It seems too bad that after all this effort the Micmacs didn't pan out too well — they took one look at paleface fighting and went back to New Brunswick by the Long Trail, not waiting for a boat ride.

Another reference is in connection with the settlement of Aroostook County, which came late in Maine's history and was actually about a century ago. The French had moved into the St. John River Valley from Acadia, simultaneously with the migration to Louisiana, but English-speaking settlers held off. One man who moved into the area of Houlton got a house built and had things in hand so he felt it would be safe and comfortable for women, and then he sent back to civilization for his wife and two daughters. A guide took them over the Long Trail, and we have the notes written by the eleven-year-old daughter as they made the journey. She didn't like it a little bit. It was a horrid experience, and she said so. She was miserable every step of the way. You wonder how she managed to come through, but then you find that her sister was only six at the time, and you wonder what an eleven-year-old was squawking about. But again, there is reference to the Long Trail.

This trail was a basic route into and from which other trails flowed and took off. One major offshoot was the Kennebec route to Canada — the one Bill Goff used to return from Quebec, and the one Benedict Arnold followed to Quebec in 1775. Evidently a good many soldiers from the Wolfe-Montcalm encounter came home that way — a number of them bringing the same story of the bombardment of the citadel, for this story is heard all over Maine as a family tradition. When the British arrived (and many of the soldiers were New England boys), they set up some kind of cannon on the shore at Point Levis and began to shoot at Quebec. Quebec stands high on the cliffs across from Levis, and so dominates the scene that the fortress looks much closer than it really is. The width of the river is deceiving, and it deceived the gunner.

So here were the English on one side of the river, and they could look across and see the Frenchmen on the parapets of the citadel, eyeing them askance and no doubt wondering just what they were up to and what they planned. Suddenly this small cannon gave off a puff of smoke, and to the English on their side it made a bang. But the Frenchmen wouldn't hear the bang until the sound waves crossed the river and all they knew was that a puff of smoke had appeared. This boded no good, so the heads on the parapet all ducked out of sight. But presently there came a splash a short distance out in the St. Lawrence River, and it was clear to all that the range had not been found. At this, all the heads came up on the parapet and the English heard a mocking Gallic cheer as the defenders of the city responded. Successively, the gunner elevated his aim and used more powder, and each time he fired, the ball would carry a little farther across the river. But each splash was followed by jeering shouts from the parapet, and the Frenchmen thought this was funny.

But after a time the gunner got in the groove, and

he dumped a cannon ball right into the citadel. No heads appeared, and there was no mocking laughter. So many young men, coming home to Maine from that expedition, told about this that it became the salient memory of the engagement, far more dramatic than the schoolbook deaths of Wolfe and Montcalm.

Another Maine story in any family with memories concerns the Long Trail walk to Boston, and the grandfather who went to the dedication of the Bunker Hill Monument. All that is necessary is an ancestor who suits the dates, because they can be isolated easily. The Battle of Bunker Hill was fought on June 17, 1775. The cornerstone for the monument was laid fifty years later, on June 17, 1825, on Breed's Hill, with Major General Marie Joseph Paul Yves Roch Gilbert du Motier, Marquis de Lafayette, wielding the golden trowel. (Bill Nye claims that at the Battle of Brandywine Lafayette had his name shot from under him three times.) The completed monument was dedicated on June 17, 1843. The prinicpal speaker at both the laying of the cornerstone and the dedication was the great Daniel Webster. So with these dates in mind you can see how remarkable is this story:

Thaddeus Bowditch Coopernail, then being a small boy, but thrown into zeal by the excitement of the times, actually took part in the Battle of Bunker Hill. This varies — some say he ran the enemy lines with code messages in cleft sticks, some say he was a water boy, and some say he really fought. But he was there, and he had moved to

Maine in the meantime, and he went back to Boston in 1825 to see Lafayette lay the cornerstone.

Moving to Maine is reasonable. Many Revolutionary veterans were given grants of farmland in Maine by the Massachusetts Assembly, and evidently some folks took up such land on thin and unchecked records. There was one soldier who had fought in the Revolution, and he came up and got a good farm. His grave is in the far corner of a now neglected cemetery, and every year the American Legion comes and puts a flag on it. A few years ago one of his descendants had the line traced, with the idea of joining the D.A.R., and the cold scrutiny of fact sort of spoiled the story. This man had indeed fought in the American Revolution, but as an English soldier, and on Bunker Hill he suffered a broken leg when some Patriot rolled down a barrel of rocks. By the time his leg healed he had become a citizen, so he came out of the woods and proceeded as stated. Maine had few Revolutionary soldiers of her own — it didn't work that way — but a good number came to Maine from Massachusetts afterward.

So Thaddeus Bowditch Coopernail had done so, and in the twilight of his life he heard with great joy that the Bunker Hill Monument was at last finished and would be dedicated on the 17th. He told everybody how he had taken part in the battle, and had gone to see Lafayette lay the cornerstone, and then he decided that he would go back to the dedication. He must go; they couldn't talk him out of it.

Doddering but excited, he started down the Long Trail.

He was wearing a pair of new boots, and scholars will want to give this full attention. In those days itinerant cobblers made the rounds and booted a whole family at once. Some came with wagons, and some carried their lasts on their backs. Anything that broke up the tedium and humdrum of backcountry living was welcome, and the cobbler brought news and gossip. He was given a bedroom, and a place by the window to do his work. He repaired boots, and made new ones if needed. He wouldn't move along to the next place until everybody was shod. And just before Thaddeus Bowditch Coopernail had set out for the dedication of the Bunker Hill Monument, the cobbler had come and had made Thaddeus a fine new pair of cowhide boots.

It wasn't many miles before Thaddeus discovered that he had made a mistake. The boots had not been broken in, and in a short time his heels were blistered right up to the nape of his neck, and he was in such pain and misery as nobody today can imagine — with mile upon mile of the Long Trail still ahead of him.

Each and every one of the Thaddeus Bowditch Coopernails came through all right. They stopped at every purling stream to lave their burning feet, and they tore the tails off their shirts to bind up their bleeding blisters. But to a man, they all arrived. They stood there, row upon row, to hear the immortal Daniel Webster, and because their feet hurt they had taken off the accursed boots and were holding each boot up under an arm. According to Maine folklore the entire audience, that day, was made up of aged Maine men who had walked down with new boots, and stood barefooted while Webster spoke.

Short-Handled Whip

Anybody going to call on a lady friend, in Maine, is likely to be cautioned to drive with a short whip, a delightful reference once you know the story. And no reason why you shouldn't, because you can hear it all the way from Kittery to Fort Kent — although my favorite is the Androscoggin County version which brings in the editorial opinion.

Rodney Pinkham was a hardworking farmer, not too settled between the ears, and he had a beautiful and charming wife who graced his home and made everything wonderful. He also had sleek cattle and profitable crops, which permitted him to maintain a very fine home, and all was well with Rodney Pinkham. However, at some stage of the game a raunchy womanizer from the village caught sight of Rodney's wife and had his desires awakened, whereat he used to take notice when Rodney was in a far field or had gone to town with some produce, and quite by chance this fellow would find some way to make an appearance.

At this point the story may go either way — half of the time she remained steadfast, but rumor grew, and at last she was unjustly suspected by her husband. The other half of the time the evil-minded old rascal from the village found her most sympathetically disposed after suitable approach. It depends on how you like your heroines, and makes little difference in the outcome of the story.

So whether the chap from the village made any hay or not, the time came when Rodney was suspicious, and one morning at breakfast he announced clearly that he was going over into the next town to look at a bull and he thought it would be a good idea to pack a lunch. His wife lamented that he would be absent so long, which he construed according-to, and off he went. He had, however, made some preparations for this trip which his beautiful wife didn't know about. He had taken the old musket down from the pegs in the shed, had loaded it, rammed in the wadding, and disposed it under the blanket in the back of his wagon. He had, actually, inserted a load heavy enough to fell a black bear. So now he laid in his basket of lunch, and a short length of rope so he could lead the bull home tied to the tailgate if he chanced to like him and buy him. He then drove off.

Instead of going over into the next town, however, he circled back at the schoolhouse, and came by a wood road back toward his own farm, and he tied the horse to a tree. He then picked up the musket and walked until he was in a clump of cedars overlooking the very road that led to his farm, and he sat down out of sight and stayed there all day. Now, whether the gentleman from the village was truly involved with Rodney's wife, or was by misluck moved to pass that way uninvolved, he did, anyway, drive by. Rodney heard the horse and buggy coming, and he looked out from his clump of cedars, and he saw the object of his suspicions clear and distinct, sitting up on the seat and looking, Rodney thought, rather pleased with himself.

At this, the coldly calculated plan of Rodney is embellished with passion and anger, and what he meant for a desperate deed is now a fearful act of vigorous vengeance. As the horse and buggy, and rider, move toward him, Rodney draws a bead down the length of his gun barrel, and he waits until his victim is directly in front of him on the road. Then he lays his thumb on the hammer and cocks the musket, and pulls the trigger.

The gentleman on the buggy seat, coming along and suspecting nothing, nevertheless reflexes well at the sound of the click when Rodney draws the hammer back. He doesn't know just what the click is, but he instantly reaches forward and whacks the rump of his horse with his whip, with the idea of getting to hell out of there. And he has a short whip.

This means that he has to lean forward more than he would if he were using a whip of regulation (retail) length. So when the musket went off, the charge did not come to where the man was, but it came to where he had been before he reached ahead to touch up his horse. It brushed the back of his neck with a deadly swoosh, but that was all. And his horse, who had no trouble feeling the whip and hearing the gun go off, lost no time in leaping into a gallop, and he went merrily away with the buggy bouncing ten feet off the road.

In the more didactic versions of this story the gentleman sees the light, and never approached Rodney's wife again. But in the version I like — the Androscoggin County version — the gentleman never had anything to do with her anyway, and was as innocent of the gossip as she was, and he now becomes mighty curious about who tried to do him in, and why. He thus returns with the sheriff, and the only clue they can find is the wadding that Rodney had used in the gun. It was the editorial page of the Lewiston *Evening Journal*, and at Rodney's home they found the very paper from which he had torn it when he loaded up. At the trial which took place, when Rodney was accused of attempted murder, the prosecuting attorney introduced the wadding as evidence, and read it to the jury. Its Republican flavor was appreciated.

But in all the versions the short whip is the constant. The man owed his life to a short whip. And when a man puts on a necktie and strikes out on an affair of the heart, in Maine, like as not some friend will call after him, "Just be sure and drive with a short whip!"

Maine Weather

It has long been customary for Maine people to invent prodigious weather, but in recent years the development of four-seasons recreation has put a crimp in the tradition. To a ski resort, snow is worth thousands of dollars an acre, and what was once considered a miserable winter day is now a valuable asset. Our official state publicists have actually suggested that the old-time tall tales of rugged Maine weather are bad for business, and as loyal citizens we should make things sound as lovely as we can. The real old claims may thus become only collectors' items, and the day of bragging about unbearable storms, as intellectual pastime, is gone forever.

The town of Pittsfield once had a poor farm and, for some reason nobody has ever explained, there were three thermometers on the porch. Now, three thermometers make excessive equipment, and that this opulence was lavished on a poor farm is interesting. But there they were, and when one of them said it was thirty below zero you could go and look at the other two, and they would corroborate the testimony. At length this gave somebody an idea, and for a number of years whenever there was a cold spell the aggregate temperature of Pittsfield, namely ninety below zero, would be announced. The Associated Press got sucked in on this a few times, mostly when they had a change in managers and a new man took over.

This was in keeping with the old way — to make weather sound as bad as possible, and embellish the cold facts until they became amusing.

"Snowed? I guess it snowed. It took me two days to sweep out what blew through the keyhole."

"Snowed? Well, I guess ... Why, I started for the barn with two empty milkpails, and it was snowing so hard I had to dump 'em out three times on the way!"

"We had a lot of snow that winter. Power failed, and the electric light company sent a crew to shovel out the line. They dug down and found a row of apple trees, so they knew they were in the wrong place."

"I shoveled the path for the first two-three storms, but after that I had no place to put more snow, so I tread 'er down."

"I took snowshoes come March and went around and tapped some maple trees. Then came a warm spell and the snow melted, and we had to collect sap with ladders."

"See out the windows? We couldn't even see out the one in the attic."

Thermometers that burst from the cold were frequently reported, and if somebody demurred that cooling mercury will never expand, the answer was, "Well, it was so cold it did that time!" This objection was also countered by stories that the mercury was hanging six inches below the glass. Another favorite was to go look at the thermometer on the side of the house and report that it was six clapboards below zero. Farmers would tell how the mercury had gone to the bottom of the glass and two feet down a hoe handle leaning against the wall. And a 33-degree Mason dropped to just four above.

"Mild winter. Fairly mild. Only went down to

minus forty-five twice, and then only a week at a
time. Shot up to thirty-eight in February, and we
had a heat wave."

"There was one night we had a teakittle of water
boiling on the stove, and it was froze solid."

This was the tendency, but now we merely say
there is an adequate base, with six inches of new
powder, and all areas are in operation. The clear,
bright, snappy morning is just fine, and gone are the
old-time observations that "I wouldn't want to haz-
ard a guess as to how cold it was, but my cow
wouldn't let me milk her without mittens on."

A Maine fog gets tiresome after a couple of weeks,
but one or two days at a time is bearable. The poet
R. P. T. Coffin rose to magnificence with his line
about a Maine fog: "And cows in pasture fade away
to bells." But a more typical reaction goes like this:

"We was shingling the fish house when it came in
to fog, and I'm telling you I never see just such a
mull as that one. We had to hang our heads right
down to the roof to see the nails at all, and the only
way I knew Charley was still on the roof with me
was, I could hear his hammer going. But we had the
job most done so we stuck with it to finish up, and
you know what happened — we shingled right off
onto that fog bank and laid the roof seventeen feet
out beyond the boards. Nailed her right down to the
fog. Next morning the fog lifted, and carried my
fish house out to sea — just left a chimney hole
standing there, and I don't mind saying I was some
put out. Worst fog I ever saw."

Often told about Seguin Light, but equally at home with any other mariner's beacon, is the story of the twenty-seven days' fog. It closed in the last week of July and hung on almost through August, a thick blanket of fog that shut out all the world and left the Maine coast mildewed and despondent. When it moved in, Leslie Bridges, the keeper of the lighthouse on Seguin Island, started up his compressor engine and set the foghorn a-going. Every minute, for ten seconds, the foghorn would blat out its warning, and such is the power of "Old Seguin" that landlubbers twenty miles inland can hear the thing. Can you imagine sleeping out on the island with the thing, and having it go off every minute for twenty-seven days?

Well, it wasn't twenty-seven days, really. It was on the twenty-third day, about half-past two in the morning, that the belt on the compressor snapped, and all at once there was no air for the horn. So at the end of the next minute the horn didn't blow, and Leslie jumped out of bed and said, "What was that?"

The allegation that Maine lobstermen have a sixth sense and navigate in bedtick fogs without compasses is gratuitous. They can get lost just as fast as anybody, and do, but being knowledgeable on the water they recover quickly, and being smart they try not to get lost in the first place. It's about like the woodsmen inland; ask a guide if he ever really got lost in the woods, honest-injun, now, and he'll have some answer like, "Well, not above a day or two at a time." It's like Reuel Hanscomb, who got lost in the snowstorm. He'd been to town, and he started the two-mile walk home just as it began to snow. It got dark, and all at once Reuel realized that he had wandered off the road, wading hip-deep in snow, that he couldn't see his own mittens, and that he was lost. He exhausted himself trying to get back on the road, and he finally leaned against a tree and felt himself slowly fading away. He knew that he was freezing to death, and this is the way it went: numb, but comfortable. A great peace settled over him, and cark and care eased away. He thought vaguely about how long it would take them to find his body. Just then a great-horned owl that had been perching out the snowstorm on a limb of that same tree gave off his whooping who-who-who right into Reuel's ear.

It scared Reuel so that he roused up and went home.

Fishermen who get lost usually finish the experience by coming home, and there is some bravado that overplays the true concern that prevailed when they were still out. Novelists have tried several times to portray the anxiety of a small Maine fishing harbor when, for a short time, somebody is missing. True, the anxiety on occasion is prologue to tragedy, but far more often it passes when off in the harbor fog a familiar exhaust is heard, and everybody says, "He's in." Then comes the bravado, and when Shorty Walpole appeared from a fog-mull a good five hours late, Henry Weston jibed at him with, "What happened — you didn't get lost, did you?"

"Hell, no! How could I get lost — I didn't know where I was, anyway."

Another time Russ Balfour guessed wrong and struck out toward Spain when he thought he was heading for Chicago, and as soon as he found his mistake he turned around and came home. Meantime the whole town was sure he was lost, and it was a wonderful moment when they finally heard his engine coming. But on the dock, when he arrived, the conversation gave no hint of the municipal concern and public apprehension:

"Couldn't see too well out there, could you, Russ?"

"No, I got to get my glasses changed."

Then comes a Maine day such as no other place in the world ever sees. Sky so high and so blue, and fair breezes. An April morning with geese wedging in, or a bright September afternoon. There never was, and you can't find, any hyperbole or deprecation of good Maine weather. The state stands mute when the good days come. It was on just such a fine day that the Massachusetts motorist drove in at Tyler Brigham's filling station in Cornville, and found Tyler sitting in the sun, his chair tilted back against the building and his hat balanced over his eyes. Tyler made no move, and the Massachusetts motorist tooted his horn. Tyler paid no never-mind, and the Massachusetts motorist tooted again. Then the Massachusetts motorist called at him in the manner of the tourist, and he said, "Hey, there!"

He finally had to get out of his automobile and walk over and shake Tyler by the shoulder, and

Tyler pushed his hat back and looked up at him.

"Well," said the Massachusetts motorist. "Don't you want to fill my tank?"

"Nope."

"Aren't you open for business?"

"Nope."

"Don't you sell gasoline?"

"Yes."

"Well — can I buy some?"

"Not today."

"Why not today?"

"Because," said Tyler, "it's too good a day. I woke up and I took one look at it, and I decided I was going to sit here and enjoy it. And that's what I'm doing, and that's all I'm going to do. No, it's too good a day to pump gas."

The Massachusetts motorist didn't seem to believe what he heard.

Tyler said, "But I was sitting here half expecting you."

"Expecting me?"

"Eyah, more or less. I bet my wife ten cents I'd no more'n get comfortable when some goddam Massachusetts driver'd show up."

Some Odds and Ends

Sooner or later every Maine compendium gets to the recipe for cooking a coot. Sometimes the original is credited to an old Indian who lived nearby, but whatever form the recipe takes, the basic inference is that nobody in his right mind would even think of cooking a coot. The truth is otherwise. A great many coot have been cooked and eaten in Maine, and coastal people adroitly prepare them and bring them to the table so they are tasty and nourishing. The coot is a much maligned creature, and is merely another duck whose flight each fall makes him available.

The coot is really the American Scoter, a sea duck who will fly twenty-five miles from one cove to another when he might have covered the same distance in a hundred yards overland. "Crazy as a coot" is therefore standard Maine judgment, and those who best know the bird often add, ". . . in a south wind." The coot does not have the same caution and craftiness of other ducks sought by hunters, and a flock of them will come to tollers set in the open ocean and fly around and around the boat anchored there until the last one has been shot. When other kinds of ducks come to tollers, there is a blind, and considerable stealth on the part of the sportsman. But when coot come in, you stand up and whistle, and wave your hat, and yell at them, and they get curious and stay for supper.

The coot is also a trifle hard to kill. When you have bagged one and brought him into the boat and banged his head on a thwart, he will get up and walk around. Being a sea duck, he has an oceangoing tang which you don't find in puddle ducks inland, and this is often called a fishy flavor. But however often the classic recipes for cooking a coot are repeated, a coot nevertheless can be prepared for table so the fishiness is resolved and the meat is juicy and tender. The illusion of toughness and rankness need not prevail if a cook is able. But in folklore, the coot remains an object of scorn.

The basic coot recipe is to lay the birds in a roasting pan, and as you arrange them for cooking you put an ax in the pan with them. Then you cook them, basting them liberally, and as soon as you can stick a fork in the ax the coot are done.

In a variation on this, you throw the coot away and eat the ax.

Another oddity in Maine affairs is the cow that ate oats. For some reason a folklore opinion became established that common oats were bad for cattle and should not be fed. Oats, of course, were for horses, and "feeling your oats" derives from the peppiness that comes to a well-oated horse. Let a horse stand in the barn unworked for a time, getting oats regularly, and the next time you take him out he'll dash around and skip and sometimes kick the buggy apart. There used to be, in Maine, a cartoon that would show up in the weekly newspapers occasionally — it showed an old fellow standing in a barn door with one hand thrust inside a bag of feed. The caption was, "Old gentleman feeling his oats." The real reason for giving oats to horses and never to cows was one of color. Evidently, in the long ago somebody did experiment, and found that a cow fed on oats gives a white butterfat which makes butter look like lard. This, in time, produced an adage, or precept, so that everybody knew that you shouldn't feed oats to a cow. Besides, the gastronomic equipment of a bossy is different from that of a horse, and rumination sets up a reaction to oats. Oats tend to swell on a cow.

However, most communities produced, off and on, some experimental soul who fed a cow oats just to find out what would happen, and in all instances the cow shortly decided she was a horse, and did all sorts of horsey things which were extremely funny, such as doing a mile in $2:07:\frac{1}{2}$. One cow was a pacer, and could run so fast that she arrived in the next town five minutes before she left home. And so on.

The student will be interested that most of this oats-and-cow lore proceeded from the oddities of the horse, and not from those of the cow. Evidently, in the old days the horse was used and endured in Maine out of necessity, and not from any sentimentality. Old farm plugs did rare and unusual things, and the more unexpected things sounded the most likely. In the town of Rangeley, years ago, a man took the job of plowing the village sidewalks after snowstorms, and he had a small sled-plow drawn by one horse which quickly cleared for foot traffic and he was faithful about getting out early and doing the job. But as time ran along he got old, and so did his horse, and year by year the sidewalk job took longer and was less well done. Indeed, motorized equipment came along, but the townspeople were kindly, and out of respect for long years of service they left this job to this man. And it so happened that after one snowstorm he was driving his plow along right in front of the post office, and suddenly his old horse keeled over and slumped into the drifts.

"Migawd," said somebody, "your hoss has dropped dead!"

The old fellow calmly surveyed the beast and said, "He never done that before."

The crux being that you really never could depend on a horse, and if he could think up something new, he'd do it. Thus the oat-eating cow who thought she was a horse presented a new way to emphasize the fact.

Dogs are important. "Smartest dog I ever see was an Airedale owned by an English professor down to Bowdoin College. You could yell 'Lay down!' and 'Set up!' at him all day and he wouldn't hear you, but if you said 'Lie down' and 'Sit up,' he'd respond instantly. Used to bark twice for a noun and three times for an adverb."

Another smart Maine dog was the one that always hunted a raccoon to size. They'd show him a skin-stretching board for a raccoon pelt, and he'd go out and find a raccoon to fit. One day the dog saw them making a board to stretch a bearskin on, and he went out and hasn't come back yet. Still looking for a raccoon that size.

Marty Broderick up to Canaan had a dog he taught to fetch firewood. Any boy can teach his dog to fetch a stick, but Marty thought that was idle effort, so he trained his dog to pick up a stick at the woodpile and bring it into the house and lay it in the woodbox. One day Marty was away and the kitchen door got left open, and when Marty came home the dog had the kitchen full of wood. Took Marty all afternoon to clear away so he could get near the stove to make supper. After that he had to teach the dog to count; taught him to stop at twenty. Dog never had more than twenty sticks in the woodbox at one time. But a sad thing happened to that dog. Marty bought a coal range, and didn't use wood anymore. Broke the dog all up. So Marty used to keep a small pile of wood just for the dog, and after the dog lugged it in Marty would carry it back to the shed. Marty was relieved when the pooch finally died. Saved them both a lot of work.

There was one fellow trained some pigs about the same way. He read in a magazine where some professor was working with pigs, and he conditioned them to respond to bells. He'd put feed in their box and then ring a bell. After a time he got them so they'd come running when they heard a bell, and then he got them so they wouldn't eat, no matter how much food he gave them, unless he made a ting-a-ling first. Well, Henry Boardman read this, and it gave him an idea. He had three shoats that had been giving him trouble by rooting out of their pen. They'd get out and roam up through the fields, and Henry had a time of it rounding them up to eat. So he rigged a sort of ladder over the fence of the pen, and he patiently taught the pigs to climb over this ladder, to eat, every time he whacked on the board with his vittle-paddle. Took a lot of time, but hogs have time. After that Henry didn't care if they rooted out or not — he'd spread the grub, whack on the board, and home would come the pigs, on the run to climb the ladder back into the pen.

Well, down the road a ways Melvin Thatcher

hired two Polacks to shingle his barn, and the minute they started hammering, the pigs climbed up on
the roof with them and created some astonishment.
Pork hadn't been that high in years. But funny as it
was, the story has a sad ending. A flock of wood-
peckers moved into the orchard, and the shoats ran
all their fat off trying to run down all the knocks.

Perley Goodsell used to have a cat he taught to
ring the front doorbell when she wanted to come in.
Kind of comical. But Perley sold his house and
moved into another place that had a big brass door-
knocker, and no bell, so he had to have an electrician
come and install a doorbell just for the cat.

And mention should be made of Bobby Knowles's
hound, which was so lazy he wouldn't run a fox unless another fox came and pushed him along.

Either an odd or an end is the story of the candidate for governor who borrowed a dory and rowed
out to an offshore island to see if he could drum up a
few votes. There had been over a week of fog, and
he found the fishermen sitting in their bait houses in
glum despair. The candidate thrust a hand forward,
and to start the conversation he said pleasantly,
"Are you interested in politics?"

The fisherman said, "I ain't interested in a damn
thing until the fog lifts."

And a famous odd, or end, concerns the elderly
woman who was slowly dying in bed in the upstairs
chamber, and her conscience bothered her until she
confessed to her husband, "Every time I was un-
faithful I put a bean in the old cookie jar on the
top shelf."

The husband went down to the pantry to investigate, and he found about five quarts of pea beans in the jar. He brought it up to the bedroom.

"Quite a few beans here," he said.

"Yes."

"Did you keep an accurate count?"

"Yes. They're all there. Except when I ran short and cooked a pot of them for a Grange supper."

A Few Inventions

Inventiveness, in general, is excellent Maine material, although often it works out something like Dr. Foster and the little stick on his buggy wheel. He perfected a device to measure distances. Every time his buggy wheel rotated, this little stick made a clack noise, and by keeping count as he rode along he could tell you just how far it was from his stable to any house in town. But the doctor became so absorbed in counting clacks that he often drove right past his patient's place, and then he'd count clacks to find out how far he'd gone by mistake.

Now our Maine paper companies, when they buy a new automobile, put it in the shop first and weld two tow bars to the frame, front and rear. There are places and situations in the far woods where this saves the company many precious hours, and it is also a criticism of the motor vehicle manufacturers, who put out cars with no tow holds on them. But this criticism was leveled, long ago, by Charley

Lovell, who decided to be an automobile mechanic back when he owned the only automobile in town. He had an early model which he fixed himself, and as time ran along he found that when he took something apart and repaired it he would have nuts, bolts, washers, and assorted items left over. His car would run just as well as, and even better than it had before, and what he was really proving was that he knew more about automobiles than the people who made them. And, as automobiles became common and he kept repairing them for people, he accumulated superfluities until one day the timbers of his garage cracked and let all his excess metal down into the cellar. Between Charley and the paper companies, you get the picture — the motor vehicle manufacturers either make you pay for something you don't need, or leave off something you want. This just about covers the subject of Maine inventiveness.

No matter what comes to hand, somebody sees through it and improves on it, and in the purple fringe of Maine folklore there is even the story of the man who invented a machine that replaced sexual relations. And then there was Lincoln Brown, who did away with the spark plug. Well, he fell to wondering one day why all automobiles use spark plugs, when there is no need to, so he took an old motor apart and studied it. Then he put it together, with a few adjustments, and he left off the spark plugs. He had a new and much better way of igniting the fuel. He showed it around, and before long a man came to his house and said he would like to buy Link's invention, and was quite prepared to make

Link an attractive offer for it. So Link sold, and has spent his winters in Floridy ever since — and that's why you always find spark plugs on an automobile engine. Well, the man who bought Link's invention had been sent up by a company that makes spark plugs.

Another motor vehicle improvement invented in Maine is the self-starter. When autos first came along they were cranked, so J. Lorenzo Bascomb, who was even better than Thomas A. Edison, thought about this, and he came up with a homemade self-starter. In fact, Bascomb made several styles of these gadgets, and at one time he had an automobile with four different self-starters on it. When you stop to think that no automobile then made had a starter, but that Bascomb was driving a car with four, you understand what a great inventor he was. People came from all around to watch Bascomb start his automobile. He had four push buttons on the dashboard, and he would select a button, and push it. After he had pushed all four buttons he would get out and crank his machine.

Except for labor-saving ideas in the original fisheries, the first important Maine invention was the set-over ox yoke. There is much lore about it. Oxen, thrusting their necks ahead into a yoke, are actually using the common lever and fulcrum, and if you let one ox get a mite farther from the center clevis than the other, the proportion of leverage is disturbed. You'd be making one of them work harder than the other. Well, in teaming with oxen, there might be a stump in the way and one ox may need to step sidewise for a moment. In order for him to do this, the other ox must step sidewise with him. But the set-over yoke was designed something like traverse rods for window curtains, so the two oxen could move closer together or farther apart without changing the point of pull. It was, truly, an ingenious device, with sliding parts, and if medicine had made similar strides the common cold would have disappeared long ago. But many amusing things happened as oxen found out about their new freedom, most common of which was to suppose that because they could step around a rock or a stump, they could step around a tree.

The set-over ox yoke led, naturally, to the set-over pung. In winter, with traffic along the roads mostly by teams — that is, by two animals walking abreast — the single-horse sleigh didn't work so well. The runners would, of course, ride where the heavier work-sled runners went, but the single horse in the middle had poor stepping. So the set-over pung was a sleigh with an offset singletree, and the one horse jogged along handily out to one side. But again, as with most Maine inventions, there were difficulties that led to lore, and with the set-over pung the common incident was when the horse, becoming preoccupied, thought he would jog a while on the nigh side instead of the off, and he pulled the sleigh along for a hundred yards or so astride a pasture fence. Another common plight came when two set-over pungs met and both horses and drivers forgot about being set over, and while the horses passed each other readily enough, the pungs tangled.

There is another automobile story heard now and then. It is the forerunner of the automatic quick-fire machine gun, and if you look it up you will find this was invented by Sir Hiram Stevens Maxim, who was born in Sangerville, Maine. When Hiram was a small boy, about 1850, there was an old fellow lived in Sangerville named Judson Hooper, who was something of an inventor. At that time the first whisperings of internal-combustion engines were being heard, and Judson worked on it. It sounded to him as if the search for a suitable fuel, which eventually turned out to be gasoline, could be answered by plain gunpowder. If an exploding substance thrust a piston in a cylinder, it wasn't going to be too different from a bullet leaving a gun barrel. Judson therefore built a four-cylinder motor which was hardly more than four shotguns lined up, and while it sounded a good bit like the Battle of Bunker Hill, it ran very well. It was a ten-gauge engine. Young Maxim, of course, saw this engine hauling a load of logs to the mill, and later in life he was to recall it when he came to invent the machine gun. As to Judson, he had the hard luck of having his spark work back into the fuel line, and the barrel of gunpowder on his back seat exploded one day between the house and the barn.

Similar outcomes prevail with Lem Gorse's bean-threshing machine and the cordwood take-away of the Bickford boys. Lem rigged four bean flails around a revolving platform, and built a windmill to supply power. It threshed beans all right and was a great thing, but one day in a high wind Lem fell into

it and suffered great indignity before he could crawl
out. The cordwood take-away was a more sophisticated machine, and eventually was perfected and
used everywhere. But when the Bickford boys first
made it there was one small bug. They had a wood-
yard and sold firewood, and they chunked up the
cordwood sticks with a circular saw that ran by belt
off a one-lung gasoline engine. In normal use, this
required three men — one to pass from the pile, one
to saw, and one to take away. Since there were only
two Bickford boys, this meant an expense, so they
perfected a device to do the taking away for them. It
was a chute with an endless chain, belted to a
countershaft, and as the sticks dropped away from
the saw they would drop into the chute, and lugs on
the chain would carry them up and off the end into a
cart body. Now the Bickford boys could saw wood
with just two, so they went about it.

The first stick, a hefty section of choice white
birch, dropped into the chute, was caught by a lug,
and immediately made a looping trajectory off over
the village and disappeared from sight. The Bickford
boys had put the big pulley on the wrong shaft, and
had increased the speed accordingly. The chunk of
birch came down at the Dobbins & Hinckley Green-
house, where Joe Dobbins and Harry Hinckley were
at that moment planting out a bed of carnations.
Fortunately nobody was hurt, but the glazing bill
was considerable. The Bickford boys reversed the
pulleys and sawed wood for years with no further
incidents.

We should also consider Tunk Coombs and his work with the doodlebug tractor. Long before motor vehicle manufacturers put a farm tractor on the market Tunk was making them for his neighbors from secondhand parts. They would plow and pull a mowing machine, and didn't cost much or stand around and eat when they weren't working, so Tunk was kept busy making them. Like a traditional Swiss watch, no two were ever made alike, and Tunk improvised according to what old parts he could pick up. You'd get a Ford front end, a Chevy motor, a Dodge transmission, and a Hudson rear end, and things like that. Tunk would shorten things up, so the doodlebug was compact. So eventually he made one for Wattles Keene, and it was something of a collector's item because it had three transmissions in it. Well, Tunk had a transmission he wanted to use, but the only gear in it that still worked was reverse. Now, if you put two transmissions together and put both of them in reverse, the thing will move forward. Tunk knew this, but to get speed he had to put in a third transmission. So when Wattles Keene came to get his new doodlebug, Tunk carefully showed him how to work the three foot levers and the three stick shifts, and by putting two in reverse and one in forward Wattles was able to drive home at a reasonable speed. But a day or so later Wattles tried to pull a stump, and when he got the chain in place he sat up in the seat and carefully thought out all the details Tunk had explained. He pushed with his foot and he worked with his hand.

He now had the thing set for slow forward speed, with great power, and then he backed into the stump at ninety miles an hour.

It would be unfair to conclude this study of Maine inventiveness on this note, for there is always to be remembered the touching story of J. Lorenzo Bascomb and his perpetual motion machine. Every town, sooner or later, had a man who invented perpetual motion, and he was always the victim of the great scientific expert who came around and told him it couldn't be done. Well, J. Lorenzo did it. He had the thing in his henhouse, and it was a great tub with a funnel-like cone rising up, and the cone had vanes on it. It was so artfully arranged that four quarts of water going down would lift five quarts up, and it ran on and on for years and years. One day a professor from Bates College came and looked at it, and he made a typically profound professorial comment. He said, "No, Mr. Bascomb — it is not perpetual motion; I think you may have made a good water pump, but that's all."

Of course, as a water pump the machine had no particular charm to J. Lorenzo Bascomb. He was perfectly capable of making a better water pump any time he pleased, and he would have approached a water pump in a water-pump mood. But this time he had started in a perpetual-motion mood, and that is what makes the difference. It is something scientists, and professors, will never understand.

Years ago there was a little farmhouse over on the east side of Mosquito Hill, where lived Henry Thompson. Henry invented a better mousetrap. It was a simple thing, and under a grain chest it would take as many as two dozen mice in one night. But fame did not come to Henry, and the world did not beat a path to his door. Back in 1919 the little dirt road that led past his home became impassable, and a sign appeared at the town line: "Road Closed, per order, Selectmen."

Some Hors d'Oeuvres

A gentleman lying abed at night listening to the activity in the swamp behind his house suddenly bethought himself of a great economic opportunity, and the next day he rushed to the local meat market and asked, "Would you like to buy ten million frogs' legs?" The moral may undoubtedly be applied to numerous human infatuations and suppositions, the outcome being that he drained the swamp and found the noise had come from only four frogs.

Some excellent folklore must necessarily fall by the wayside as the frame of reference changes and the early-day commonplaces become mysterious. Witchgrass, a coarse and thickly rooted hayfield item, is best understood by those who in the long ago tried to cope with it in a garden with a simple hand hoe. This led to the fine story of the man who dug a well and said he went down thirty-five feet and found witchgrass roots, but no water. Similarly lost, probably, is the meaning behind the exchange:

"You better hurry over to your brother's — he's met with a great loss."

"What happened?"

"The mice girdled all his alders."

Nobody much today will understand what an alder tree, or bush, amounted to back then, but if mice had girdled every alder in Maine it would have made farmers happy, and there was amusement in considering somebody so far down the scale of poverty that losing his alders would be considered a loss. Equally humorous then, and equally unhumorous today, is the story of the farmer who approached the fish factory at Milbridge and asked if they'd like to buy some alder wood — a story in the same vein as the ten million frogs' legs. Alder is used for smoking alewives and herring. They agreed to buy four carloads, and the farmer went home and started cutting. The humor lies in the farm-bound understanding of alder wood — you can cut ten acres of alders and then push the wood home in one wheelbarrow load.

There is a legend about the man at North New Portland who made the best fox bait in Maine — but, again, full appreciation comes only if you know what fox bait was, how it was made, and how it was used. In a gallon glass bottle, usually by secret formula, a man would age choice oddities. A bit of cheesecloth would be tied over the top to keep flies out, and after the sun and hot summer had done their work you could smell this upwind for ten miles. A drop of it on the pan of a steel trap would attract a fox from three counties away. This man up at

North New Portland had a secret formula that was much better than any other secret formula, and he sold his bait to trappers in little medicine bottles — like rare perfumes and vintage wines. The story may be drawn out to any length and embellished with many a detail, but the upshot is that he forgot where he had aged a bottle of this precious stench, and one time it rolled off a shelf and burst on his head. The story goes that foxes would come at night and bark under his bedroom window.

Long before horses became mainly a western privilege, there existed all over Maine a waif of a yarn about the gentleman, often a minister of the gospel but always a sedate and mannerly citizen, who rode horseback over to the next town to pay court to a lady. Since it was something of a canter, he took a change of clothes along in a saddlebag, and just before he approached the lady's home he meant to shift out of his travel-tarnished suit into a fresh one. The story revolves around his changing his pants in the saddle. Somewhat astonished at the commotion this created up on his back, the horse took off in wild flight. The gentleman, of course, rides pell-mell past his ladylove in an unclad condition. If modern folklorists don't fully appreciate this, they might try changing a pair of pants on horseback.

A lovely old story is told on Win Smith, at the time a farmer on the Mere Point Road out of Brunswick. Win was a graduate of Bowdoin College, and once a year would dress up so he looked like a pious Presbyterian preacher, and he would attend commencement and carry himself like a scholar.

But at all other times he studiously played the part of an untutored Maine farmer with special effects for the many summer complaints who came to Mere Point from far places. Win sold them butter and eggs, and cut their grass, and the last thing any one of them would ever have suspected was that Win could have translated the Latin on his diploma. So, one winter Win was horribly gored by his bull. The animal suddenly went mad, and caught Win between the wall and the tipcart, and he nigh killed Win. Win was hurried to the hospital and patched up, and it was months before he could do much more than move his fingers.

But come summertime he was on a rocker on his porch, his feet up on the railing, and he was describing his misfortune to one of the summer ladies. He didn't leave out a single agony. At the end of his recitation the summer lady said, "Good heavens, Mr. Smith, whatever did you do with the vicious brute!"

Win struck an attitude of conquest and said, "I et him!"

Another good story about Win is the time a busload of Coast Guard sailors, bound from Baltimore to Rockland, took a wrong turn and bogged down in a mudhole in front of his farm. The driver, who had never been in Maine before, stepped up to Win's front door and inquired if Win had anything that would pull him out. Win did, and he brought down his farm tractor with a chain, and he hooked on.

Then he shut off the engine and said to the driver, "That'll be a hundred dollars."

"I don't have any hundred dollars, and a hundred dollars is too much, anyway — unhook, and I'll get somebody else."

"You can't," said Win. "Law of the sea; salvage law. I got a line on her first, she's mine. Nobody else can touch her."

"You damn fool," said the driver. "Salvage law is no good here. She's a bus, not a boat!"

So Win said, "Then how come she's loaded with sailors?"

The reference to a "hog on ice" is often misunderstood. "As independent as a hog on ice" is a standard Maine remark, and usually brings to mind the thought of a pig sliding around on a frozen pond — which is wrong. A pig can't stand up on ice, and is anything but independent there. The real meaning of the reference comes only to those who remember how a pig was slaughtered on the farm in the old days. After bleeding, he was dipped in scalding water to start the bristles, and after the bristles were scraped off he had to be cooled, not only to reduce body heat quickly, but to overcome the effect of the hot water. A good way to do this was to lay him out on a couple of cakes of ice. Now, the expression taken on by a deceased pig is one of utter complacency, and as he lies there cooling, the independence of a hog on ice becomes evident.

Slaughtering hogs gave rise to another basic Maine story. On the farm children had few toys, but when a hog was killed they could tie a string on his bladder and have a football. Whenever Father announced that he was planning to stick a hog tomorrow, the children would "hosey," and the bladder would go to the first one who cried, "I speak for his bladder!" For a few days, at the most, this made a toy, and kicking a pork bladder around was the closest old-time farm children ever came to the organized recreational programs of our day. The folklore story, thus, comes from the very poor farm family, away back over the hill, who had nothing except a great many children. Fourteen, usually. And one night the house is very still, for one of the children is ill. Mother and Father are at the bedside, and the thirteen other children are sitting about on chairs in the kitchen. At length the father comes out of the bedroom, his face set, and he says, "Children, your brother William is dead."

Whereupon everybody yells, "I speak for his bladder!"

Another old-time Maine story that needs old-time understanding is about the game warden who stopped a lady hunter and inspected the two deer she had shot. In those days it was legal to take two deer in Maine in one season, so she was all right on that score, but the warden was suspicious when he found both deer had been plugged right between the eyes. About a hundred times out of a hundred, if you find a deer cleanly shot between the eyes it means jack-poaching — the animal is found at night with a flashlight, and while he stands hypnotized by the glare in his eyes, the poacher drops him. Otherwise, normal daytime hunting would seldom give a hunter that same kind of a shot. So here was this woman with two deer, both looking very much poached, and the warden got a mite nasty about it.

The lady protested her innocence, and said she had found the deer standing in a clearing about four hundred yards from her, at high noon, and she had shot them between the eyes because they had happened to be looking her way. The warden humphed at the four hundred yards, and one thing led to another until the lady said that if he would set up his nice gold Hamilton watch in the crotch of a tree four hundred yards away, she would prove that she could hit it.

Well, you don't hear so much about them now, but in those days the different firearms-and-ammunition people used to have professional crack shots who traveled about giving exhibitions. This lady was, of course, Annie Oakley in her only known Maine appearance, and the next week the game warden received a fine new gold watch in the mail, courtesy of Remington, or Winchester, or Savage, or whatever it was that was sponsoring Annie at the time.

Another Maine poaching story of widespread application is about the traveling salesman who arrived home in some Boston suburb, after a week in Maine, and found the trunk of his automobile full of fine moose meat. Moose meat was then, and is now, highly illegal, and as the salesman reflected on his trip he did remember that about everywhere he had gone in Maine he would glance up and see some game wardens looking at him. He had no idea where the meat came from, but it was good, and he ate some and he gave some to all his friends.

On his next trip to Maine, every time he stopped to make a sales call somebody would step up and ask him what he did with all the moose meat. It turned out that everybody in Maine had known the meat was in his car, except him. The answer is elementary — some poachers had the meat, and when they realized the wardens were closing in on them, they parked beside the salesman's car and transferred the meat to his trunk, after which they drove off. The wardens now knew where the meat was, but they also knew the salesman wasn't the poacher. So they figured the real poachers would appear, sooner or later, to get their meat back, and they simply tailed the salesman all over Maine. But the poachers were smarter than that, and the salesman hauled home enough Maine moose meat to feed half of Brookline.

Bear stories are a dime a dozen, but they, too, usually depend on some knowledge of bears, which few non-woodsmen possess. The bear is mostly nocturnal, extremely fast and elusive, and many a veteran woodsman will tell you he's never seen one except on a dump or in a trap. If a man goes hunting in Maine and returns to Trenton, New Jersey, with a tall story of how he shot a vicious bear that was charging him, he's probably a cock-eyed liar, and he bought the bear for five dollars from some farmer who caught him in a trap in the pigpen. The best way to test my statement is to look at all Maine bears that go to New Jersey and see which foot is mangled.

Ed Grant had one story about the fine bear he trapped. Because he didn't want to make a bullet hole in such a beautiful pelt, he starved the bear a few days until he got thin inside his hide, and then he teased the bear with food until he walked right out his own mouth and left his hide whole on the ground behind him. Ed told it much better than I do, but it took longer.

But perhaps the favorite Maine bear story is about the hunter from Connecticut who came up with a party, and while the others played cards in camp, he announced that he was going out and get a bear. He found a bear, and the bear charged him. The hunter ran, and the bear kept on his heels. So the hunter headed for camp, and burst in the front door, and his cronies looked up to see what was going on. The bear came in.

As the Connecticut hunter escaped by the camp's back door he yelled, "Here's one! Take care of him, and I'll find another!"

Or, in a less improbable version, it goes that the Connecticut hunter, stealthily making his way through the woods looking for game, happened to glance back, and he saw a great black bear less than ten feet behind him, sniffing at his footprints in the snow. The hunter said, "You like the smell of my tracks? OK, I'll make some more."

And Caveat Emptor

Sharp trading has not only been recognized for its economic nuances, but in Maine it has a high entertainment value and is conducted somewhat on the same cultural level on which other people go to baseball games and play bridge. It is perfectly true, as reported, that my grandfather and Horace Jordan "made their livings selling things to each other," and although each suffered inglorious stickings from time to time, neither ever got mad about it, and both knew how to retire gracefully and think up a way to get even.

Perhaps the salient consideration in studying this trait of Maine people is indicated by the story told about Pete Newell. Pete was, at his zenith, the top man at the Bath Iron Works, a ship-building corporation with worldwide fame, but he attained this position by hard work and good thinking, for he was born a poor boy. When he was a boy he came into possession of a derelict sloop which, after his first interest ran out, lay in the mud in Camden harbor and was a dubious asset. However, it turned out she was really an original Muscongus type, and time had given her value as an antique. Along came a man who recognized the lines, knew what she was, and he approached Pete with the idea of acquiring her and restoring her.

Pete, already knowledgeable although still young, said he didn't know if he wanted to let her go or not, and the dicker began. In the end Pete let the man have the old wreck, and in payment he received a hundred dollars in cash, a lot in the cemetery, a horse and buggy, a sleigh with extra harness, a pair of field glasses, a set of shoemaker's tools, an icebox, a tennis racket, an emery wheel, a sewing machine, a dining-room set, and a jackknife.

Somebody who heard about this felt that the final jackknife was something of an anticlimax, so he asked Pete why he had held out for it. Pete said, "I just figgered I ought to get all I could."

The jackknife, however, should not be dismissed lightly as an anticlimax. There is another story, heard all over Maine, about the fellow who went to the fair, and because he had no money for a ticket he climbed over the fence. But he was a trader, and shortly he found something he wanted, and he traded his jackknife for it. Then he was in business, and he spent the day swapping and trading, always getting a little boot, and by evening he was in good shape. He not only had his jackknife back, but he drove home behind a span of horses hitched to a hayrack, and in the rack he had a good many farming tools and household items, besides ten sheep, and he had a bull tied to the back end. It is pretty hard to find a boy or man in Maine who can't fish in his back pocket and bring out a jackknife; it is not only a handy implement, but it is just as good as money in the bank.

Along with the raffle of the dead horse and how to stop a horse from drooling, one of the commonest Maine stories is the horse trade where the owner says, "He doesn't look so good, but he's a fine animal."

After the trade the victim returns to say, "You cheated me — that horse is blind!"

The answer is, "No, I didn't cheat you — I told you plain and fair that he didn't look so good."

One of the stories about my grandfather and Horace Jordan is the time my grandfather got Horace to buy a horse. Grandfather said, "This horse has two faults. I'll tell you one before we trade, and if we trade I'll tell you the other."

Horace said, "What's the first?"

Grandfather said, "He's awful hard to catch."

There would be a very simple answer to this fault — if he's hard to catch, then don't turn him loose. So Horace said, "All right, I'll take him — what's his second fault?"

Gramp said, "He's no damn good when you do catch him."

A good instance of sharp trading is told on Booker Douglas. He used to operate around Bowdoinham, and was considered highly as an astute member of the self-employed profession. One year he bought up the whole delinquent tax list in Bowdoinham. There is a new system now, under which towns take tax liens, but in those days property on which the tax remained unpaid was auctioned off in April. If you bought any of this property at the sale, the town would give you a thing called a tax deed. Because the delinquent owner could come in and redeem his land, these tax deeds weren't much good. They weren't even as good as a quit-claim deed, and they were by no means up to a real warranty deed. Consequently, there was never much traffic in delinquent tax property at these sales, and the town itself would bid in the list and then sit back and wait out the redemption period.

Well, this year Booker Douglas came in, and to everybody's surprise he bid off the whole list, handed over the money, and he said to the town officials, "Now, to save you time, I've got the deeds all made out here — all you have to do is sign them."

Well, Booker Douglas had prepared warranty deeds for all the property, and the selectmen presumed erroneously that he had prepared tax deeds. They didn't trouble to read them. This misfeasance came to light about six months later, when some poor farmer showed up at the town office and said, "I finally got the money together, and I'm here to redeem my property."

The story goes that when they approached Booker Douglas he said, "Redeem *what*?"

Brice Booker, no particular relation to Booker Douglas, likes to tell of the time Will Jordan bested him in a small matter. Will had a portable sawmill, and one day he moved it to a new location. Brice, who is not noted for coming out second best in a business transaction, noticed that a lot of odds and ends were left on the old lot. Some slabwood, a couple of piles of waney boards, some odd timbers. There was quite a bit that could be salvaged. So Brice approached Will and said, "What'll you take if I clean up the lot?"

"What would you think it's worth to you?"

Brice said, "Oh, I'd give you ten dollars."

"Aye-yes," said Will, which was an expression with him, "that seems fair, go ahead."

So Brice put a truck in, and he got fifteen big loads of various kinds of lumbering rejects on which he could turn a penny, and did. So he was in the bank one morning and saw Will, and he said, "I got that lot cleaned up, Will, and I might's well pay you now."

"Aye-yes," said Will, "did you find anything worth hauling away?"

"Quite a good bit," said Brice. "I got fifteen truckloads in all."

"Aye-yes," said Will. "Now, let's see — fifteen truckloads, and that was at ten dollars a load . . ."

Brice protested that it was not at ten dollars a load, but ten dollars for the whole lot, but Will said, "I distinctly recall our agreement, man to man . . ."

Brice always said that he paid Will a hundred and fifty dollars because the deal had been a good one even at that price, and he'd made a penny on it. He said it wasn't worth fighting over. But Brice likes to conclude this story by citing the unfair advantage Will Jordan took of him afterwards. "He died before I could get even," says Brice.

It would take a Solomon to draw the line between some instances of Maine sharp trading and the more open varieties of thieving and stealing. Judge Louis A. Jack, in his time a wise and discerning justice, tried to draw this line once and failed. It had to do with Mintie Guptill, who had his own sharp-trading abilities, and liked the traffic in wood and hay.

Mintie had an old white horse and a wagon. He also had what is sometimes called "vocabulary flux" in Maine — the ability to talk with the longest words available. No matter how small the topic, he would roll out magnificent conversation. Other people would remark that it was raining, but Mintie would say, " In all modesty, with respect to my meteorological prognostication proclivities, I would conjecture and asseverate a considered opinion that precipitation is prevailing." Mintie's wagon tipped over on him in the village one day and he was pinned under a wheel, and he began to yell, "Extricate me! Extricate me!" This mannerism of his is important, because it had a disarming effect — instead of listening to what Mintie said, everybody would listen to how he said it, and he could insinuate a peripheral semantic until you wouldn't believe it.

His simplest stunt was to drive into a dooryard when he knew the man of the house was away, and he'd begin loading firewood into his wagon. If he wasn't discovered he just drove off, and he had a load of free wood. If the lady of the house came out, however, he would feign astonishment and say he had come to pick up the firewood he had bought from her husband. "I am confronted," he would say, "with the presumption that your connubial mate has not confided in you that I have purchased a quantity of arboreal fuel!" Sometimes the lady would fetch a shotgun and drive him off, but Mintie's luck held up over the years, and he often drove away with his load.

Mintie didn't get caught with a load of stolen

wood aboard, because he artfully disposed of it immediately. He would drive into another yard, knowing this man was away, too, and he'd tap on the door with his whip until the lady appeared. "Good morning, Madam," he would say, "I've conducted thither the cordwood your husband ordered — That'll be five dollars."

Mintie worked the same scheme on loose hay, and sometimes vegetables, and once he did it with a hive of bees. But one day he was caught red-handed, and the sheriff waltzed him before Judge Jack with more evidence than he needed. Mintie whimpered a good deal, promised to reform and mend his ways, and begged for understanding sympathy. Judge Jack gave him a stiff lecture, and then said, "All right, I'm going to hold off the jail sentence, and put you on probation. But if I get another complaint, I'll have you picked up, and you'll get the full sentence." Mintie thanked the judge and said, "I assure you you'll never regret this kindness."

So a few days later Judge Jack came home in the evening from his office, and he found a load of firewood piled on his back lawn. "Oh," his wife said. "Mintie Guptill brought it — he said it was his way of thanking you for being so kind to him."

Which made the judge feel good, of course — except that the next Sunday after services the judge went over to his little back woodlot where he liked to work up firewood for exercise, and he found that the pile he had cut the previous Sunday had been stolen.

Rolling off a Log

The old-time Maine river driver with his spike-sole shoes joined the dodo and the auk long since, but in his day he built up a wealth of both fact and legend. His job was to herd the mountains of long logs from deep in the wilderness, down the swollen springtime streams, to the mills. On the move, with the wangan and the cooks trying to keep up, he danced around on the timber to make sure it didn't snag and jam, and his calk-boots gave him foothold. The river driver stood tall, and the best way to understand his lore and legend is to go to the city of Bangor and stand before the statue erected there — it shows three powerful river drivers hard at it, cast in perennial bronze.

When a drive came downriver and hit a town, the desire for frivolity was always hard on dance floors. The river drivers had only their calk-boots, and if they were to dance they had to dance in the calk-boots. This was good in a way, because there is no record that a calk-shod Maine river driver was ever swung off his feet in a Lady of the Lake, but the steel spikes riveted through the soles of his hi-cut heavy boots did not improve the floors. This led to a statute, duly enacted by the Maine Legislature, making it a serious offense to wear calk-boots in certain public places such as dance halls, hotel lobbies, railway cars, and so on. A howl went up, because this was clearly discrimination, and for some time the topic was touchy. It shows, however, that the calk-boot was common enough so it became a statewide menace to parquetry and such.

Today the calk-boot is a museum piece. Just a few years ago the Worumbo Woolen Mill needed to do some repair work on its dam, and the men found they needed some calk-boots to negotiate the slippery timbers underwater. By paying the long price and waiting three months, they could get such boots from a shoe factory that would make them to order. But the dam work had to be done at the seasonal slack pitch of water, so they couldn't wait. Leo Thibodeau of the woodlands department of the Great Northern Paper Company learned of this, and he lent some boots to the Worumbo. Leo wrote, "Be sure and keep them well greased and return them carefully in good condition, because they are valuable antiques and we intend to preserve them for their historical value."

Thus the Maine river driver has vanished.

When that law was passed making it illegal to attend a dance and rip a floor to pieces with spike-sole boots, the river drivers "rigged a scheme." They would take a grain bag, known also as a gunnysack, and wrap it around each boot and tie it with twine. Thus the spikes were rendered docile and no harm came to the floor. These massive bindings were known as ballet slippers.

In addition to miles of prose legend about river drivers, the Maine saga has a great deal of back-woods verse on the subject, and a good part of that

verse has to do with some river driver who rode a log over a falls, or down some gorge, against impossible odds. In the 1920's Hollywood did a film based on the Holman Day novel, *Rider of the Kinglog.* As usual, most of the work was done in California, but for authentic Maine scenery a camera crew came to the town of North Anson and filmed a few sequences there in the white water of the rocky gorge on the Carrabasset River — sometimes called the Carry-m'-basket. The wedding scene at the little white church on the hill was easy enough, but to effect pictures of the manly hero, with calk-boots and long pickpole, tousing down the current on a spruce log, an elaborate system of guy-ropes and cables was arranged. The hero couldn't have fallen off the log if he had tried. In those days Maine still had plenty of spring drives, so quite a batch of real river drivers came to watch the movie version. It was said that over fifty men who could have ridden the log in their sleep stood on the bank and sweat blood for the hero — they were afraid he'd get tangled in his safety gear and snap his neck.

Just about the time long log drives began to fade from the Maine scene, something possessed Flats Jackson and Bibbie Rundell to go on a trip. They were excellent woodsmen and lifelong river drivers, but they hadn't seen much of the country, and they took off. They had no destination in mind, except that they planned to be back in Maine by the time chopping started again in the fall, and one pleasant summer afternoon they chanced into a little town in Minnesota where the annual mammoth celebration was taking place. There was a parade, barbecue, and all manner of fun. And in the afternoon on the pond by the park there was a birling contest to find the champion birler of Minnesota.

The only thing about birling that was new to Flats and Bibbie was the name. It turned out to be log-rolling — two men would hop on a log in the water and try to twirl the log until one of them fell off. Flats and Bibbie liked that, and after they had watched a few Minnesota challengers go into the drink, they borrowed some calk-boots and had at it. The contest wound up with Flats and Bibbie on the same log, and they twirled away at each other and had a wonderful time. Along in the late afternoon the crowd got tired of it and went away, and finally Flats and Bibbie hopped ashore and returned their boots. They appeared to be the champions of Minnesota.

But there was a man there, and he said, "I can use you if you're interested. I put on the acts at the sportsmen's shows, and you fellows could do the birling act in the tank. There's a week's pay in it."

"'Beats working," said Flats, so he and Bibbie signed up and went on tour, and their first job was in Chicago. They came out on the stage, and there was a fanfare from the band and a big introduction, and they hopped on the log in the tank and began to birl. They got the log going one way, and then they bit their great steel spikes into the bark and got it rolling the other way, and it was a real fine demonstration of a very special talent. But again, after a while the crowd moved along, and when Flats and

Bibbie jumped off the log the man came up to them and said, "What's-a-matter, you two guys crazy in the head or something?"

Flats and Bibbie thought they'd done fine, so they asked the man what he was sore about, and he said, "Why'n hell didn't one of you fall off?"

Flats said, "What would one of us want to fall off for?"

"Because the crowd expects it — that's what they pay to see!"

"Look," says Flats. "Bibbie and me learned to ride logs back in Maine, and he couldn't twirl me off and I couldn't twirl him off — we just don't fall off."

"Well, you do here — and if you don't, you can pack up and go home to Maine!"

So after that Flats and Bibbie took turns, and every performance one of them would fall off and make a crowd-pleasing splash, and they had a wonderful time. But after they got back to Maine they would tell about it, and almost every time somebody would say, "How in the world would you manage to fall off a log?"

And Flats would say, "Well, 'twarn't easy."

The Tale of the First Cat

[The late Prof. Sigmund Weeps of the Department of Speech, University of Eastern Arizona, isolated this excellent example of Maine folklore at Five Islands, while at the Tukey cottage on a ten weeks' grant. Mr. Ralph T. Godbout, a humorist with considerable local reputation, put the story on tape.

Because of Prof. Weeps's protracted illness and
early demise, the story was never transcribed for the
folklore publications, and this is its first appearance
in book form.]

Far down the dim and misty corridors
of time, in the antedated, antiquated, post-amor-
phous period, there dwelt over in the town of Bowdoin (in back of Carter's Corner and just east'ard
of the Fisher Brook bridge) an aged sage with a
perfectly enormous saturation of knowledge, and his
name was Mortimer W. Gillespie and he had a hole
in his door, for the cat.

It is necessary to relate at this time that the cat, as
a separate and integrated unit, had not at that time
been invented, but Mr. Gillespie, in the abundance
of his circumspection, had foreseen the eventuality,
and he knew that a near neighbor with a flair for
ingenuity was working on the idea.

This neighbor had red hair and was named Balthazar Hanscomb, and the quantity of his inventions
was prodigiously immense.

In those long-ago days, considerably previous to
the present, the arts and sciences were scarcely heard
of, and most people went around suggesting that
Balthazar Hanscomb was something less than
bright, and they frequently ridiculed him when he
went into Ryder's store for groceries. In fact, it was
not at that time generally supposed that Mortimer
Gillespie, even, was overgifted, and the hole in his
door for the cat was everywhere considered the
greatest single piece of absurdity yet contrived.

One evening Harry Mathewson dropped in to

neighbor with Mr. Gillespie, and, seeing the hole in the door for the cat, by way of making talk, he said, "I see you have a hole in your door."

Mr. Gillespie replied that, as Harry had observed, he did have a hole in his door. "It's for the cat," he said.

Harry leaned forward and said, "For the what?"

"For the cat," said Mr. Gillespie. And he added, "A cat is a feline animal."

"Good heavens," said Harry, "a varmint?"

"Not necessarily," said Mr. Gillespie, and he expounded on the advantages and faults of the species, if and when one should be invented, and he explained carefully that (if the invention were a success) the cat would want to come in and go out with an independent whimsy that would, without a hole in the door, prove bothersome to those who kept one. Harry waggled his head and said, "It appears to me that the idea is sound, but how soon do you expect the cat is going to be invented?"

"That," said Mr. Gillespie, "is a matter of time only, and has no important bearing on the fact that one will, someday, be invented. Balthazar Hanscomb," he said, "is working on the idea."

So word went all over the town of Bowdoin, and even up into Litchfield and Webster, that Balthazar Hanscomb was working on a cat, and although few people regarded the fact as important, all were interested. Some people would say, "What is a cat, anyway?" And about the only answer was the dubious assurance that it came in and went out through a hole in Mortimer Gillespie's door, and this tended to send the community into spasms of laughter. For something like seventeen years Bowdoin was a very happy town, and everyone chuckled a good deal about Balthazar Hanscomb, who was making a cat to come in and go out through the hole in Mortimer Gillespie's door. Mr. Gillespie all the time (because of his immense erudition) smiled knowingly to himself, and this led people to fancy he enjoyed the joke as much as they, and everyone looked pleased and happy, except Balthazar Hanscomb.

Mr. Hanscomb, who refused to comment on the progress of his many inventions, was evidently having difficulty with the cat. He would come out of his shop every now and again, leading some new and interesting creature with a string, and people would crowd around and ask if *that* was the cat. The truth was that Mr. Hanscomb never knew just what he did have, and he wouldn't know a cat, anyway, and the only way he could find out was to go over and ask Mr. Mortimer Gillespie, who knew everything and was extremely intelligent.

One day he would come up with something, hoping that at last he had made a cat, and Mr. Gillespie would shake his head and sigh. "No," he would say, "not yet. You have invented the horse, my friend, but not the cat." Another day Balthazar would come again, and Mr. Gillespie would sigh again and shake his head again and say, "No, not yet. You have invented the weasel, but not the cat."

Mr. Hanscomb might well have grown despondent over such a continued succession of unfortunate mistakes, but he was too big a genius to fret, and he would throw back his head manfully and say, "Very well — I shall try again." And he would go back in his shop and work some more on the idea of the cat.

In time this made Mr. Hanscomb's barnyard an unusual sort of place. In addition to a cow, two horses, three sheep, a goat, seven hens and a rooster, two ducks, and a peafowl — which he kept for family use — he eventually had an addax, a water buffalo, some edentates, a gemsbok, a nilgai, two quaggas, a curassow, a capybara, a coypu, some upland plovers, a vicuña, a yak, two zebus (a big one and a little one), a jerboa, a keitloa, a koodoo, an okapi, an oryx, a tenrec, scads of wapiti, and a sulphur-bottom whale.

And as time went on, the prospect of his inventing a cat seemed to be more and more remote, because hardly any of his inventions were the same size as the hole in Mr. Gillespie's door. Mr. Hanscomb gained some notoriety from his inventions and was highly regarded for his versatility, but he remained sad and determined, and continued to work on the idea of a cat. People who came to see the many inventions in his barnyard would have praised him, but he was always locked in his shop, pounding away at his bench or cranking on various machines. When they saw him come out with a new invention on a string, they would crowd around and ask if *that* were the cat, but somehow the idea of the cat never turned out right. Mr. Gillespie would sigh and shake his head.

Mr. Hanscomb invented the coach dog, the jackal,

the friarbird, the platypus, the badger, the bison, the dugong, the hoopoe, the mongoose, the musk ox, and the opossum. But the cat for the hole in Mr. Gillespie's door was still to be invented, and public opinion at last held unanimously that both Mr. Gillespie and Mr. Hanscomb were wasting their time.

But as Mr. Gillespie had foreseen all along, the time came when Mr. Hanscomb made a cat. It was on a Tuesday, and almost suppertime, when Balthazar came down the street and went up to Mr. Gillespie's front door. This new invention, on the string, was certainly the right size, and people gathered to see if Mr. Gillespie would approve. Mr. Gillespie came out of his house, took one look at the new invention, and grasped Balthazar warmly by the hand.

"Allow me to congratulate you!" he shouted ecstatically. "You have done it! You have invented the cat! After all these years! Wonderful!"

And people noticed that the cat went in through the hole neatly, and then came out again. And then it went in again, and then it went out again. And everybody could see that the hole in the door was truly a magnificent provision when it comes to cats, and they burst into a cheer. "Bravo!" they cried. "Three cheers for Balthazar Hanscomb, who has at last invented the cat!" Then they gave three cheers for Mr. Gillespie, too, who had thought up the idea of a hole in the door. It was a most happy occasion.

But Mr. Hanscomb did not appear joyous. He stood on Mr. Gillespie's steps watching the cat go through the hole, and then turn around and come out again, and then go in again. Finally, the inventor, with a sob in his throat, spoke.

"Are you sure," he asked Mr. Gillespie, "that *that* is a cat?"

"It certainly is," beamed Mr. Gillespie, "and no doubt about it."

"Well," said Balthazar Hanscomb. "I don't think it was worth the effort."

Acknowledgments

The nature of this work makes tracing origins more than difficult. Although all the stories originated long ago, some few have appeared in print within recent memory. "The One-Man Army," although extant since 1775, was published and copyright by the now suspended Boston Sunday *Post* in the thirties. "The Tale of the First Cat" is reprinted with permission from *The Christian Science Monitor* of November 18, 1944, and was copyrighted that year, all rights reserved, by the Christian Science Publishing Society, of Boston. The story of the ghost who saws wood is reprinted with the permission of *Yankee* magazine, of Dublin, New Hampshire. And probably all the other yarns, tales, and lore have appeared in print somewhere at some time in some form. If further acknowledgment is due, it is hereby gratefully presumed.